Back on the Coastal Path. Towards Golden Cap.

Long Distance Footpath

The Illustrated Guide

Steven Crockford

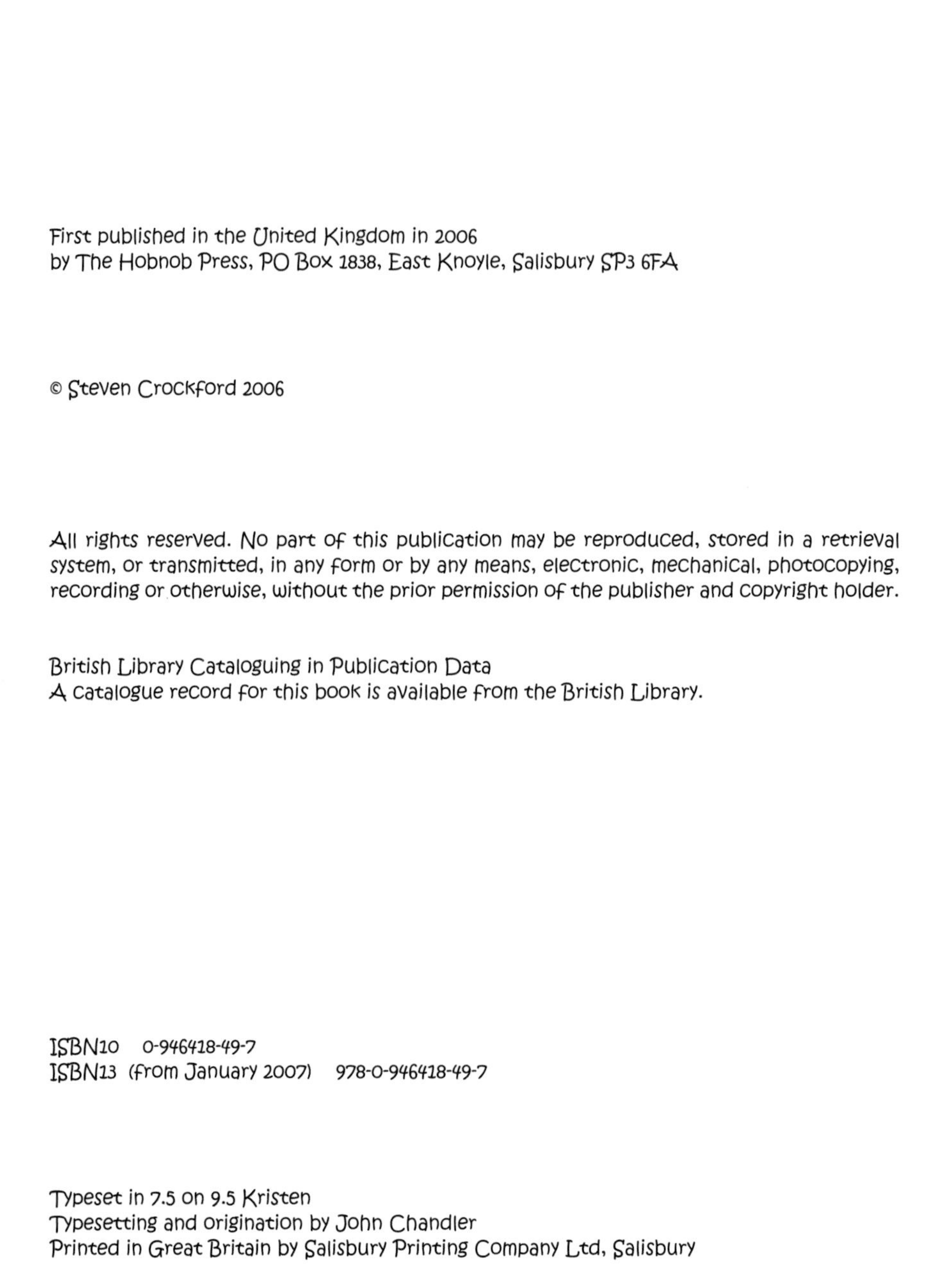

First published in the United Kingdom in 2006
by The Hobnob Press, PO Box 1838, East Knoyle, Salisbury SP3 6FA

British Library Cataloguing in Publication Data
A catalogue record for this book is available from the British Library.

ISBN10 0-946418-49-7
ISBN13 (from January 2007) 978-0-946418-49-7

Typeset in 7.5 on 9.5 Kristen
Typesetting and origination by John Chandler
Printed in Great Britain by Salisbury Printing Company Ltd, Salisbury

'We shall not cease from exploration
and the end of all our exploring
will be to arrive where we started
and know the place for the first time.'

From 'Little Gidding', Four Quartets by T.S. Eliot

Somerset
Shaftesbury
Wiltshire
Sherborne
Stalbridge
Ashmore
Sixpenny Handley
Cranborne
R. Avon
Hampshire
Yetminster
South Perrott
Evershott
Mosterton
Pilsdon Pen.
Cranborne Chase
Blandford Forum
Wimborne Minster
R. Stour
Blackmore Vale
Devon
Marshwood Vale
Christchurch
Charmouth
Bridport
Wareham
Poole
Bournemouth
Dorchester
Start
Finish
Abbotsbury
Upwey
Osmington
Lulworth
Corfe Castle
Swanage
Weymouth
Durlston
Kimmeridge
Anvil Point
St Aldhelm's Head
Portland
Durdle Door

A Round Dorset Walk

Stages

Start Point: Sandbanks, North Haven.

	Destination	Total Miles	Facilities
1	Hengistbury Head	9	T.
2	Matchams Lane	17	
3	Woolsbridge	24.5	
4	Cranborne	32	B+B V.S.
5	Sixpenny Handley	39	B+B V.S.
6	Farnham	42.5	B+B
7	Ashmore	51	
8	Shaftesbury	57	B+B F.C.
9	Marnhull	65	B+B V.S.
10	Stalbridge	68	B+B F.C. V.S.
11	Sherborne	76	B+B F.C. V.S
12	Yetminster	81.5	V.S.
13	Evershot	87.5	V.S.
14	Corscombe	92	
15	Winyards Gap	94.5	
16	South Perrott	96	B+B ?
17	Mosterton	98	
18	Drimpton	101	
19	Marshalsea	109	
20	Charmouth	115	B+B V.S. F.C.
21	Seatown	119	
22	Eype	121	
23	West Bay	122	B+B V.S. F.C.
24	Burton Bradstock	124	V.S.
25	Abbotsbury/Portesham	132/134	V.S. B+B
26	Upway	139.5	B+B.
27	Osmington/Osmington Mills	144/145	B+B V.S.
28	Lulworth	151.5	B+B V.S. F.C.
29	Corfe Castle	161	B+B V.S.
30	Kingston	163	
31	Worth Matravers*	169*	
32	Swanage	173	B+B V.S. F.C.
33	Studland	178	
34	Sandbanks, South Haven	181	FINISH.

*..... Off Route

The Maps

In preparing the route descriptions and drawing the route maps I hoped to provide such a comprehensive and understandable guide that, using the two together, even the most inexperienced map reader could set out each day confident of safe arrival at the correct destination. However, even in the seemingly benign environment of Dorset it is not hard to find yourself walking for hours in remote countryside without refuge or support,. Never underestimate the effect of changing weather conditions.
Being lost is not a pleasant experience at any time, especially towards the end of a long and tiring day. (Remember, with a map and compass, you are never lost; you just might not be quite where you thought you were!) It is my strong advice therefore that as part of your preparation for the walk you read the notes carefully, and get accustomed to using them alongside the route maps, hopefully one will make up for the shortfalls of the other. I have endeavoured to ensure that the corresponding notes and maps are on the same double spread and that you do not need to keep flipping over the page. (Always inconvenient, especially if the guidebook is inside a map-case!)

As with all 'corridor maps' they are only of value if you do not stray from the designated route. For that reason alone it is advised that you also carry with you an Ordnance Survey Map and be able to use a compass as the need arises. Not only will they help to avoid you becoming totally lost, but they will also furnish additional information that will surely enhance your enjoyment of the walk. E.g. "What is that hill in the distance?"
The maps in this guide are not substitutes for Ordnance Survey maps, they are merely memories and impressions of my journey round Dorset. Though I have endeavoured to ensure that these memories and impressions are as accurate as possible, where inconsistencies between the two occur then I defer to the Ordnance Survey; they have more experience and certainly better resources than I.

The entire route is covered by the following Ordnance Survey maps: -
1:25 000 Explorer Series. **OL 15** (Purbeck & South Dorset)
1:25000 Explorer /Outdoor Leisure Series. **OL 22** (New Forest)
1:25 000 Explorer Series. **118** (Shaftesbury & Cranborne Chase.)
1:25 000 Explorer Series. **129** (Yeovil & Sherborne.)
1:25 000 Explorer Series. **117** (Cerne Abbas & Bere Regis.)
1:25 000 Explorer Series. **116** (Lyme Regis & Bridport.)
And back to 1:25 000 Explorer Series. **OL 15** (Purbeck & South Dorset)

A complete selection of Ordnance Survey Maps can be found on the website:
www.ordnancesurvey.co.uk/leisure

The route maps are always orientated such that north is towards the top of the page.

The distances shown are cumulative and fairly accurate, though they do not allow for any climbs or descents. Other scaling is approximate, especially the width of any road or track. {On my scale, the A354 is no wider than a farm track but hopefully no confusion should arise.} The contour lines are again approximate and are intended only to suggest the type of ground to be covered and climbs to be encountered, and to give an idea of the surrounding topography.

Key to the Maps

Symbol		Meaning
— · — · —	....	Main Route
— — — —	....	Other Footpaths
43m.	....	Cumulative Distance
	....	Metalled Road Surface
	....	Wide Tracks and Trails
	....	Fence Line and Field boundaries
140	....	Approximate Contour Lines
	....	Railway Line
	....	Conifer Woodland
	....	Broadleaf Woodland
	....	Grassland, Heath or Scrub
	....	Marshy or Boggy Ground
	....	Cliffs and Escarpments
	....	Tumuli
	....	Earthworks and Barrows
†	....	Church
	....	Pub
T.	....	Tea Room or Café
P	....	Car Parks
P.C.	....	Public Conveniences
	....	O.S. Trig Point
F.B.	....	Foot Bridge
	....	Farmland
	....	Caravan and/or Camping
	....	River
V.S.	....	Village Shop
F.C.	....	Fish and Chip Shop

'A Round Dorset Walk'

Alfred Wainwright completed his 'Coast to Coast' route and guide book in 1972. In his conclusion he wrote, 'I would feel I had succeeded better in arousing interest for the planning of private long-distance walks if the book induced some readers to follow their own rainbows end.'

In consideration of that hope, I imagine Wainwright would not be disappointed by the plethora of walks and guide books his example spawned. Bearing in mind his own personality however, I dare to suggest he, of all people, would have found something to complain about. It was then, in risking his displeasure that I set out to follow a rainbow of my own, to walk around the county I call home and to record the journey in this guide. In doing so, I cannot help but dedicate it to the man who inspired it. I may not hope to equal his work, but let it be said that this guide is 'in the style of Alfred Wainwright, 1907-1991.'

There will forever be debate and disagreement as to the relative merits of one county over another. Cumbria has its lakes and fells, Yorkshire its dales and moors and Cornwall its tors, moors and coastline. Such a debate might however overlook the little county of Dorset. If it did then it would be guilty of overlooking a precious jewel. Dorset has been described as the forgotten county, but not forgotten by lovers of the writings of Thomas Hardy or of unspoilt countryside, rolling hills, lush valleys, glorious views, dramatic coastline and two hundred and fifty million years of history. Far be it from me to suggest that Dorset is in any way pre-eminent over those other counties, they, and others, offer their own unique charms. Let me suggest instead that you come with me on a very special journey around a beautiful and often-unexplored part of Britain and you can be your own judge. I respect your judgement.

The route I suggest is not 'The Round Dorset Walk'; it is 'A Round Dorset Walk'. It will use the county boundary only as a reference and not seek to follow it slavishly as that would mean missing out on some wonderful walking. Nor will it delve into the heartland to explore all that Dorset has to offer, for to do that would turn this walk into one of epic proportions. It will recognise rights of way and avoid road walking wherever possible. If however, in preparing to walk around Dorset you decide to 'do your own thing' and adopt an alternative round Dorset walk, then be my guest. (I know Wainwright would applaud you, but then he always was cantankerous – bless him!)

At something like 185 miles Dorset may not seem like such a small county after all, and it is no small challenge to undertake in one effort, especially if two weeks constitutes a drain on ones annual leave, not to say the patience of a demanding family. Instead you might like to divide the journey into manageable sections. A warning however, rural Dorset, many miles from the usual tourist haunts, is not well blessed with public transport. If lifts cannot be found, it may require imagination and advanced planning to get from start to finish, or vice-versa.

I plan to start the journey on the 'northern' side of the narrow channel at Haven Point, (crossed by the Sandbanks Ferry) and to travel in an anticlockwise direction. I do this so that one of the 'jewels in the crown', that is the Coastal Footpath, remains to be savoured. The rather less rewarding march along the promenades of Poole, Bournemouth and Boscombe (not without their own appeal, it must be said, for those with the time to tarry) is then accomplished on fresher legs. On the way we will follow a route along the Avon Valley, through Cranborne Chase and the Vale of Blackmore, to the rolling chalk hills of Marshwood Vale in the west and so to the coast at Charmouth. Here we will begin the concluding drama which is the coastal path itself, returning at last, weary but wiser, to the southern side of Haven Point. There your ferry awaits, so no point getting your feet wet unless, in time-honoured fashion, that is your intention. Having first wetted your boots on the northern side of course, (This may be especially poignant for those 'Coast to Coasters' amongst you).

Sandbanks Ferry. South Haven.

So, if you have made all the necessary preparations, arranged your accommodation, purchased (and broken in) a sturdy pair of walking boots (you will need them), paid particular attention to the "important planning note" below and finally girded your loins, lets get going.

Important Planning Note.
*Lulworth Cove To Kingston.

The section from Lulworth to Creech Hill (overlooking the village of Steeple) on the Purbeck Ridgeway, involves crossing **military gunnery ranges** that restrict access to the coastal footpath for much of the year.

This will necessitate planning your itinerary so as to arrive at Lulworth cove on a weekend or to coincide with other open periods during which access is permitted. These usually include 'high days and holidays'. The month of August is generally also a period during which the ranges are open.

In all cases I strongly recommend that during your planning, you telephone the range office on **01929 404819** to get full information. You can leave a message and they will telephone you back if you require any further details.

If all else fails and the range walks are closed to you, you will need to take the much longer, less interesting inland route, most of which will be on the minor roads. If it is in the evening, and, if the road through the ranges from East Lulworth to Steeple, (via Ridgeway Hill) proves to be open, then at least the diversion will not be too costly in terms of mileage or time. Otherwise it may require a lengthy diversion around Coombe Keynes, East Stoke, East Holme and Stoborough.

Combining, as it does, quite stunning views with places of interest such as the 'fossil forest', the Mupe rocks, the delightfully named Bay of 'Arish Mell', Flowers barrow (a hill fort balanced on the cliff edge overlooking Worbarrow Bay, and the romantic abandoned village of Tyneham', (not to mention an array of shelled tanks and military vehicles), this section is certainly one of the more beautiful and fascinating parts of the coastal walk and all efforts should be made to include it in your route.

It is easy to grumble about the restrictions and the inconvenience that they sometimes impose, but there have been some advantages for the walker. The army have been active in isolating and maintaining this part of Dorset such that it remains a haven for rare plants, birds and animals. It is free from all development and provides a walk that will live long in the memory for its unrivalled beauty and peace. Don't miss it.

Haven Point – Hurn Forest (17 miles)

The start of our journey must begin at the Sandbanks ferry (North Haven Point), with an extended promenade along the holiday beaches of Poole and Bournemouth. To those accustomed to being at the seaside, or anxious to reach the more rural hinterland of Dorset, this will seem a tedious 9 miles and will be taken at pace in order to get it over and done with. (I must confess to being amongst their number).

Yet this fails to recognise the plus points of this stretch of coast to the Round Dorset Walker. The opportunity to stretch the legs and get some miles under the belt with no concerns over route finding, the extended views across Poole Bay both forward and back to the Purbeck coast, and the availability of refreshment etc, make this an ideal first day's walk. Poole Harbour and its secret treasure that is Brownsea Island make this an atmospheric starting point, but I promise it gets better!

The 'Castle', Brownsea Island.

(A look to the southwest will be hard to resist, for there, just a short distance across the channel lies our ultimate goal. Only 180 miles stand between us!)

So lets get walking and it does feel good to be under way at last.

First make for the southeast corner of the car park alongside the ferry. A climb over the wall leads to a path between limestone boulders and the walls of the neighbouring residences. Some of these boulders have been skilfully carved; the 'handstone' will certainly catch the eye. From here the route is clear, on sand or tarmac, to the headland of Hengistbury Head in the distance. This, with its promise of views inland and green walking, will remain our goal and carrot for the next 9 miles.

The Start

The promenade is studded with 'chines', charming tree-lined access points to the coast. At each of these, and at the piers, there are cafes, shops and public conveniences; it will be a long time before such amenities are so plentiful again.

Note the cliff lifts, or funicular rail cars, that carry bathers to and from the beaches along this stretch of coast, rare indeed to find three together. The earliest two have been carrying holidaymakers since 1908.

Bournemouth Pier.

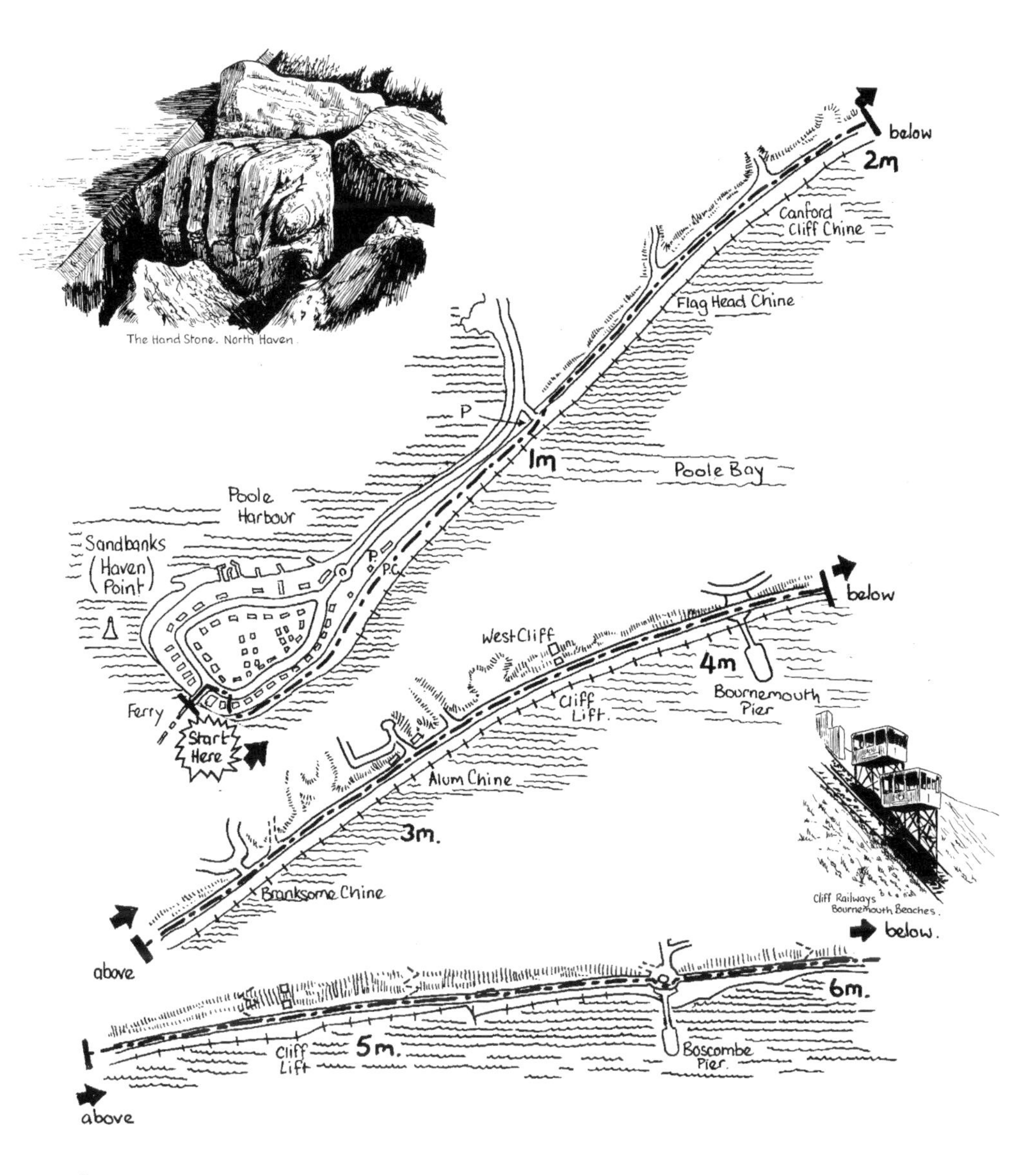

Bournemouth, as a town, can trace its origins to 1810 and specifically to a retired army officer named Lewis Tregonwell. In addition to building his home on this stretch of coastline, he planted the pine trees that line the valleys (known as 'chines'), which provide access to the beaches - thoughtful of him really.

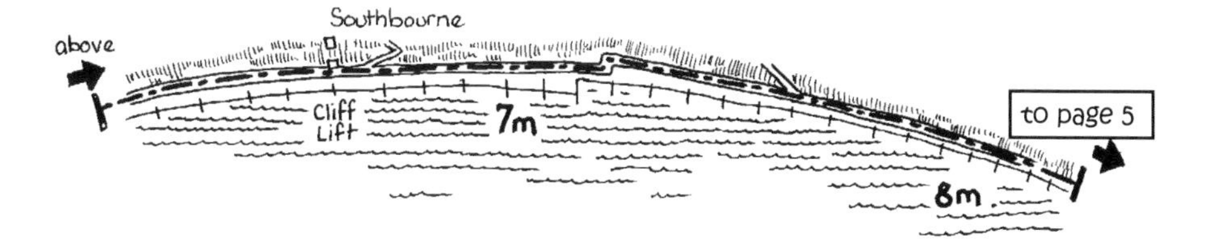

When, just beyond 8 miles, at Southbourne, the promenade finally comes to an abrupt end, climb a flight of steps to the left that emerges by a beach café. Turn to the right and join the track along the top of the low cliff towards Hengistbury Head. Extensive grassland to the North permits views across to Christchurch with the Priory increasingly prominent. After ¾ mile, this path meets with the Iron Age defence system known as 'Double Dykes'. Here you may take a clear track that heads left, in front of the earthwork, towards a land-train station and café. All subsequent mileage will be based on the assumption that this is the route you have chosen.

Hengistbury Head.

Hengistbury Head however, will reward those who resist the left turn and explore the ground beyond. Even just a short walk up the clear path to view the distance already covered, and to gain a first clear view northwards towards Dorset's heart, will be ample compensation for the effort. Hengistbury Head is a little haven, with a complex of hidden paths and delights that will absorb an afternoon for those with the time to spare.

If that is the case, I would suggest walking along the beach to the groyne at the far south-eastern corner of the headland. From there continue round the eastern end along the path to the beach huts. A stepped path climbs the hill and a range of paths can be taken back to the northern end. All routes provide wonderful views.

Whichever course you take, make your way back to the turning area on the road next to the café and there, turn to the northeast away from the coast, and go up the narrow metalled road until you meet the entrance to the Marine Training Centre. A kissing gate, ahead and to its left, offers a way across Wick Fields in company with the Stour Valley Way. Use this and follow the path out of sight of, but alongside, the united forces of the Rivers Stour and Avon, shortly to meet their journey's end at Mudeford.

After a couple of stiles and a small bridge over a creek, you enter an open area with horses grazing. Keep to the right of the field, and in twenty yards or so take the path to the right. After two gates, continue to follow the path as close to the River Stour as you are able, alongside the 'Tuckton Gardens' and the pleasure boats, until you meet the road by Tuckton Bridge.

Turn to the left, and then right at the roundabout. Take the second turning on the right called 'Iford Lane'. In one miles time turn right into Old Bridge Road. This will bring you to Iford Bridge and an opportunity for refreshment.

The Old Bridge at Iford.

Cross the road alongside the pub (The Bridge Tavern') and begin walking to the right. Before crossing the river Stour, take the footpath on the left alongside the river, an attractive and peaceful haven that will bring you, in less than ½ mile, to a golfing footbridge across the river. Walk across and turn to the left. Follow the bank past the golf course and weir, then across a playing field to a cul-de-sac by a private caravan site.

Turn right and cross the road ahead (River Way) into Stour Way. Take the next left into Hurn Way and walk to its end, and the busy Hurn Road.

The Weir. R. Stour near Iford.

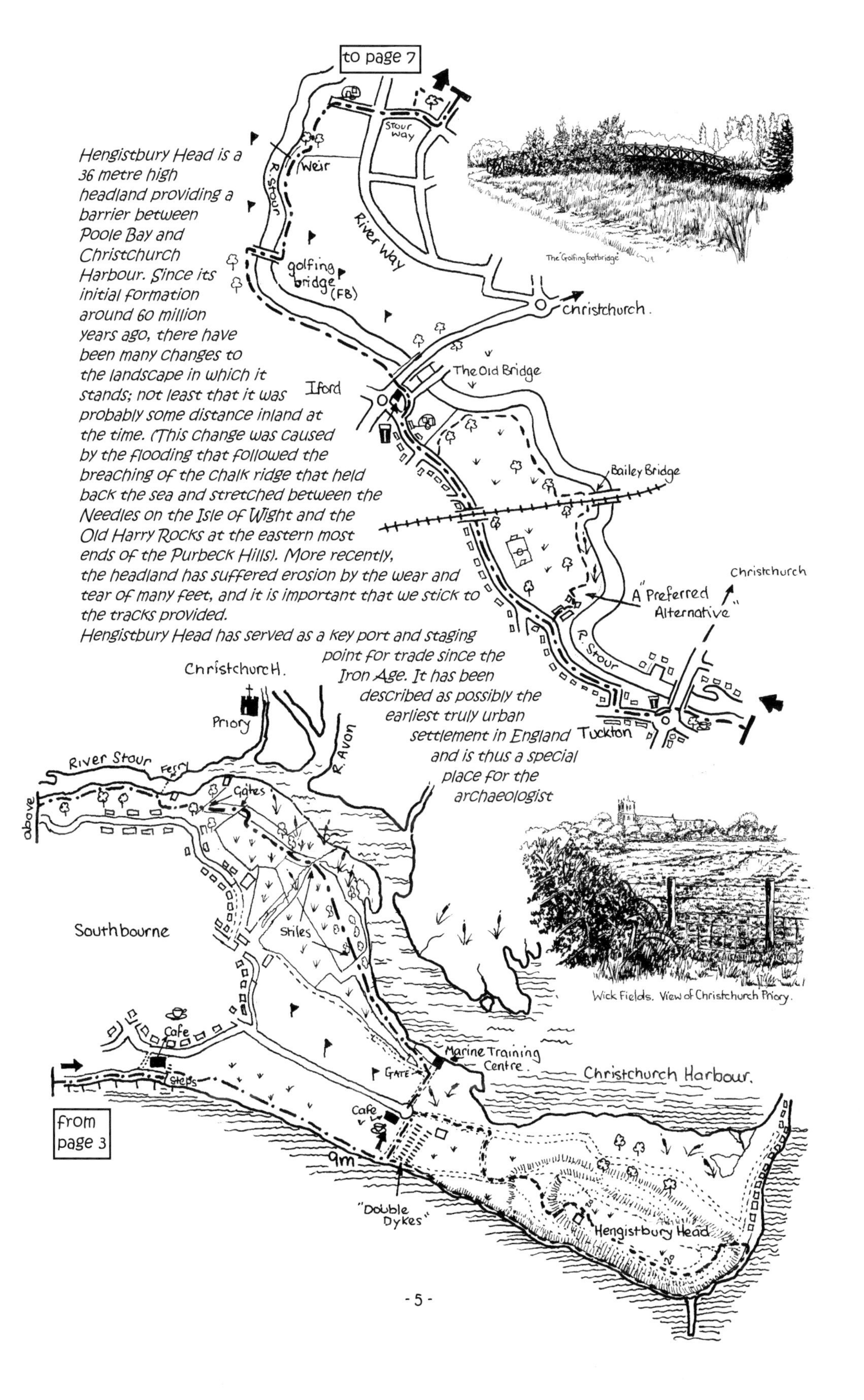

The "Golfing footbridge"

Wick Fields. View of Christchurch Priory.

Hengistbury Head is a 36 metre high headland providing a barrier between Poole Bay and Christchurch Harbour. Since its initial formation around 60 million years ago, there have been many changes to the landscape in which it stands; not least that it was probably some distance inland at the time. (This change was caused by the flooding that followed the breaching of the chalk ridge that held back the sea and stretched between the Needles on the Isle of Wight and the Old Harry Rocks at the eastern most ends of the Purbeck Hills). More recently, the headland has suffered erosion by the wear and tear of many feet, and it is important that we stick to the tracks provided.

Hengistbury Head has served as a key port and staging point for trade since the Iron Age. It has been described as possibly the earliest truly urban settlement in England and is thus a special place for the archaeologist

A Christchurch Excursion.

Although the town of Christchurch is almost by-passed by our route, it non-the-less affords a convenient halting place for those who consider 12 miles to be adequate for the first day and plan to take the walk round Dorset at a more leisurely pace. That being the case, this historic town will afford all we need for a comfortable night. There is no lack of accommodation and there are shops, cafes and public houses in plenty.

The history of Christchurch can be traced back, as a Saxon settlement, to at least the 10th century, and the reign of the King Alfred the Great. It was named Tweoxneum (meaning "the place between two rivers"), a name derived from its enviable position between the Rivers Avon and Stour. Its ancient title can still be found in the name 'Twynham' associated with its school, a church and a host of associations, gift shops etc. Its location at the estuaries of these two great rivers of Wessex made Twynham, or Christchurch, strategically important in the defence against Viking attack.

Christchurch Priory

After the Norman Conquest the town became increasingly important as a defensive position and place of worship. Construction of its Priory Church (amongst the most grand in the country) was begun in 1094, and Twynham Castle, standing on its artificial mound or motte, was established alongside it. By 1160 a domestic building known as Constable's House was constructed within the wooden palisade of the castle, and the wooden keep was rebuilt in stone by 1300. The Priory church and the remains of the Castle, and the grounds surrounding them, fully reward an afternoon's exploration.

The finest way to approach Christchurch is via the little ferry that crosses the Stour from the 'hamlet' of Wick. This lies alongside the river Stour between Wick Fields and Tuckton. Once over the ferry, turn to the right and make your way alongside the river towards the Priory. If, as is likely, the ferry is not running, continue to the bridge at Tuckton and there turn right. Take the first turning on the right after the bridge and then return to the river after 150 yards by turning right alongside a small car park. Turn left and make your way to the Priory.

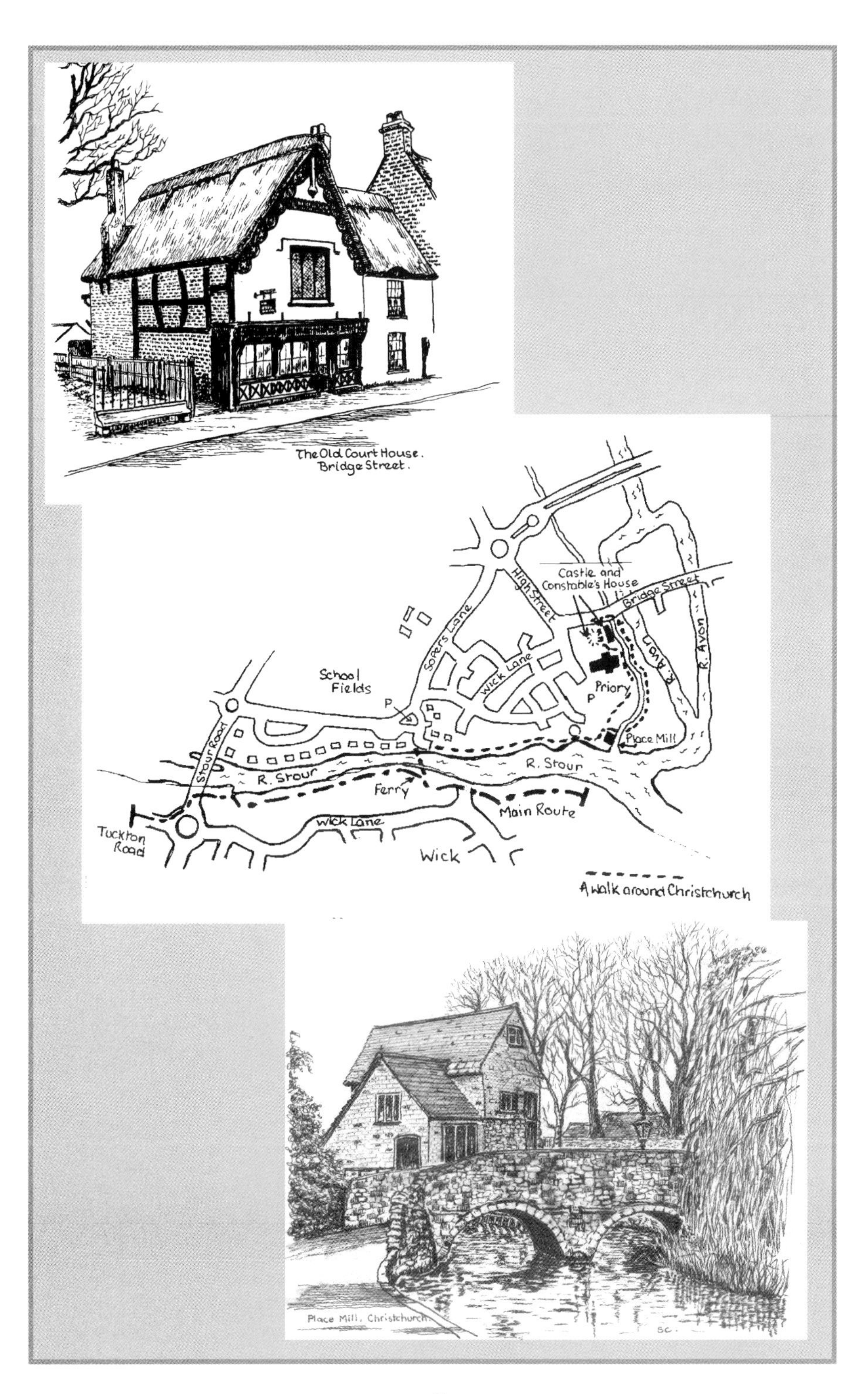
The Old Court House.
Bridge Street.
Castle and
Constable's House
Bridge Street
High Street
Sopers Lane
Wick Lane
School
Fields
P
Priory
P
R. Avon
R. Avon
Place Mill
R. Stour
R. Stour
Stour Road
Ferry
Main Route
Wick Lane
Tuckton
Road
Wick
A walk around Christchurch
Place Mill, Christchurch
SC.

Cross Hurn Road carefully through the gap ahead on to the service road and turn right then left on to Hillside Drive. As the road turns to the left, there is a green area ahead. Walk clockwise around this looking for a gate ahead that provides access to St Catherine's Hill and the end of busy roads at last.

The water storage tanks.

On emerging from beneath a canopy of rhododendrons, turn to the left for a couple of hundred yards. When you come to a broad track heading up the hill to the right, turn up it. Beyond two massive concrete water tanks, it meets the bridle path that runs along the top of the hill. Turn left and follow the bridle path through pine trees. (It is worth taking a minor detour at this point to skirt the disused gravel quarry to the east of the main track. It provides more extensive views across heath land and the Avon Valley.)

After three 'down and ups', the main path reaches the end of the Hill and turns to the left, but a bridleway continues through a gap ahead and down a steep sandy path. This is our route. The track makes a slow turn to the right around a large and ancient tumulus before heading northeast across the heath or Town Common. After a hundred yards or so, the sandy track meets with a gravel track - a dismantled railway. Take a left turn and chug along to its end and the Avon Causeway Road. An ex-railway station at this point now finds service as a public house and may well require a visit for those with a mind for railways or whatever!

Approaching the 'steep sandy path'.

Refreshed, leave the Avon Causeway to the west and cross the busy A338 via the road bridge. Shortly after take the marked footpath to the right on to Sopley Common. Whether by following the paths round the hill to your left, or by ascending it by an obvious sandy track, the way to its northwest corner will be easy to find. At a bar gate onto Matcham's Lane turn right and, keeping to the verge, walk ½ mile past the flight path of Hurn Airport, and the two well-appointed campsites on the right (The Mount Pleasant Touring Park and the more creatively named 'Portview' – the port in question being the airport!)

On reaching a Forestry Commission car park on the left, turn into Hurn Forest. A choice awaits you here. Either follow the main path ahead, which makes a beeline through the forest for the next 1½ mile, or cut right to join the lesser, but preferable path that skirts the forest alongside the fence and Barnsfield Heath. If this is chosen it will rejoin the main track a mile ahead. (Both are shown on the sketch map).

St Catherine's Hill and Town Common act as a natural barrier between the urban sprawl of the Christchurch/Bournemouth conurbation and the more rural Avon Valley.

It seems that some time in the Tertiary period this region was part of a complex of rivers feeding into a Grand Solent River (where the Solent itself is now). Sand and gravel that had been laid down was sculptured into the hill by the action of the two rivers flowing on either side of it i.e. the Stour and the Avon. Apparently Hengistbury Head was formed in the same way and thus St Catherine's Hill is a good picture of what Hengistbury Head would have looked like 15000 years ago.

Legend has it that this was originally to be the site of the church that became Christchurch Priory, but divine intervention decreed otherwise, the building materials being repeatedly relocated to the site alongside the River Avon. Whatever the truth of that, the Hill has clearly been a place of veneration over some period of time, as the many earth-works and barrows that litter the area testify.

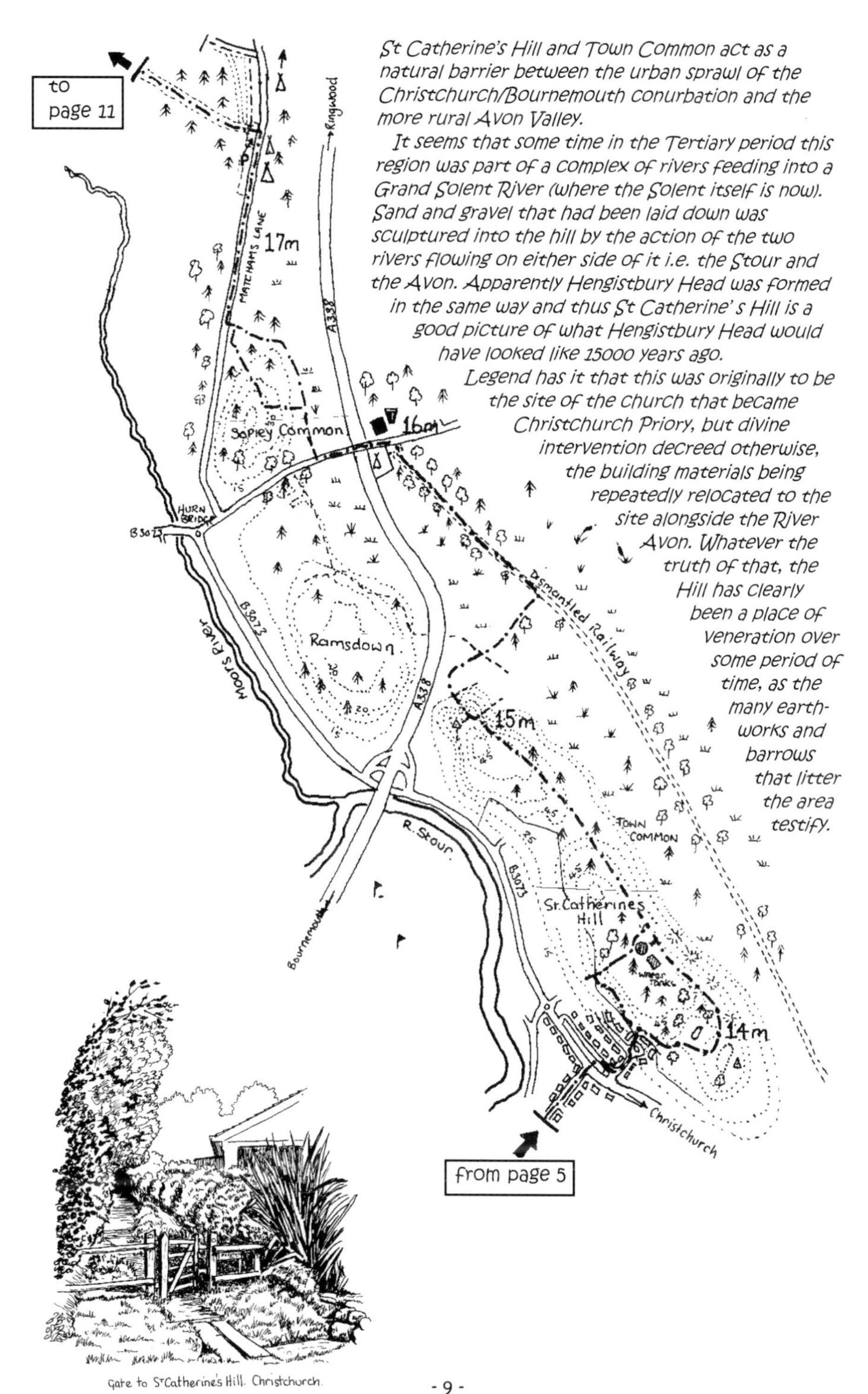

Gate to St Catherine's Hill. Christchurch.

Hurn Forest to Verwood (9 miles)

Hurn Forest exhibits the characteristics of a well-managed plantation combining financial motives with aesthetic and environmental awareness. This section is peaceful and retains interest. The next two miles will be covered quickly.

As the main gravel track turns to the right, follow it avoiding the left turn to a farm and the smaller track ahead. Beyond the point where the track curves to the left take a less well-used track at 11 o'clock to the main track. (284°) These lesser tracks are always subject to change in a Forestry Commission plantation.

Barnsfield Heath
Hurn Forest.

(If there is any doubt, continue on the main track and refer to the sketch map, you won't go far wrong! The main track ultimately reaches its conclusion on Boundary Lane. On arrival at the lane, turn to the left and walk to the junction of the A31 and turn to the left to the footbridge where you will join the original route. (See below.))

In ½ mile a caravan site will be reached. Turn to the right, and then make the next two left turns on smaller but obvious tracks. The second of these emerges opposite a high fence, which is the rear of St. Leonard's Hospital. Now turn to the left and, at the next track on the right, follow the path as it zig zags to meet the road alongside an estate of less-than-mobile homes. By now the traffic noise of the frantic A31 will be heard. Turn right to pass an industrial unit and stop at the trunk road itself. A safe crossing should be made at the footbridge 100 yards to the right.

The surroundings are far from tranquil and in spite of the pub nearby (The Hungry Poacher), walking pace may increase to seek quieter refuge.

This is not immediately apparent. There seems little alternative but to head left alongside the A31, past the pub, roundabout and lay-by and turn right into a suburban road and comparative haven, on the right, that is Abbey Road.

Take the second turning on the right (Uplands Road), and continue a short distance alongside peaceful bungalows until, when the road turns to the left, a short cul-de-sac on the right (Edgemoor Road) reveals a green Forestry Commission gate, here a clear track heads into the West Moors plantation of Ringwood Forest. Pine trees abound, but in spite of their ranks and columns, the occasional planting of hardwoods, and use of open spaces, has allowed a forest floor of grasses and shrubs to flourish and the walk is a pleasant one. Any of the smaller tracks to the right can be taken to skirt the woodland on its right to give views across the Moors River clearing. Otherwise keep walking straight ahead, avoiding obvious turns to the left until you reach the perimeter fence.

Keep the main fence line on your right as the track begins to turn to the left in a north-westerly direction.

Forestry Commission Gate onto West Moors Plantation

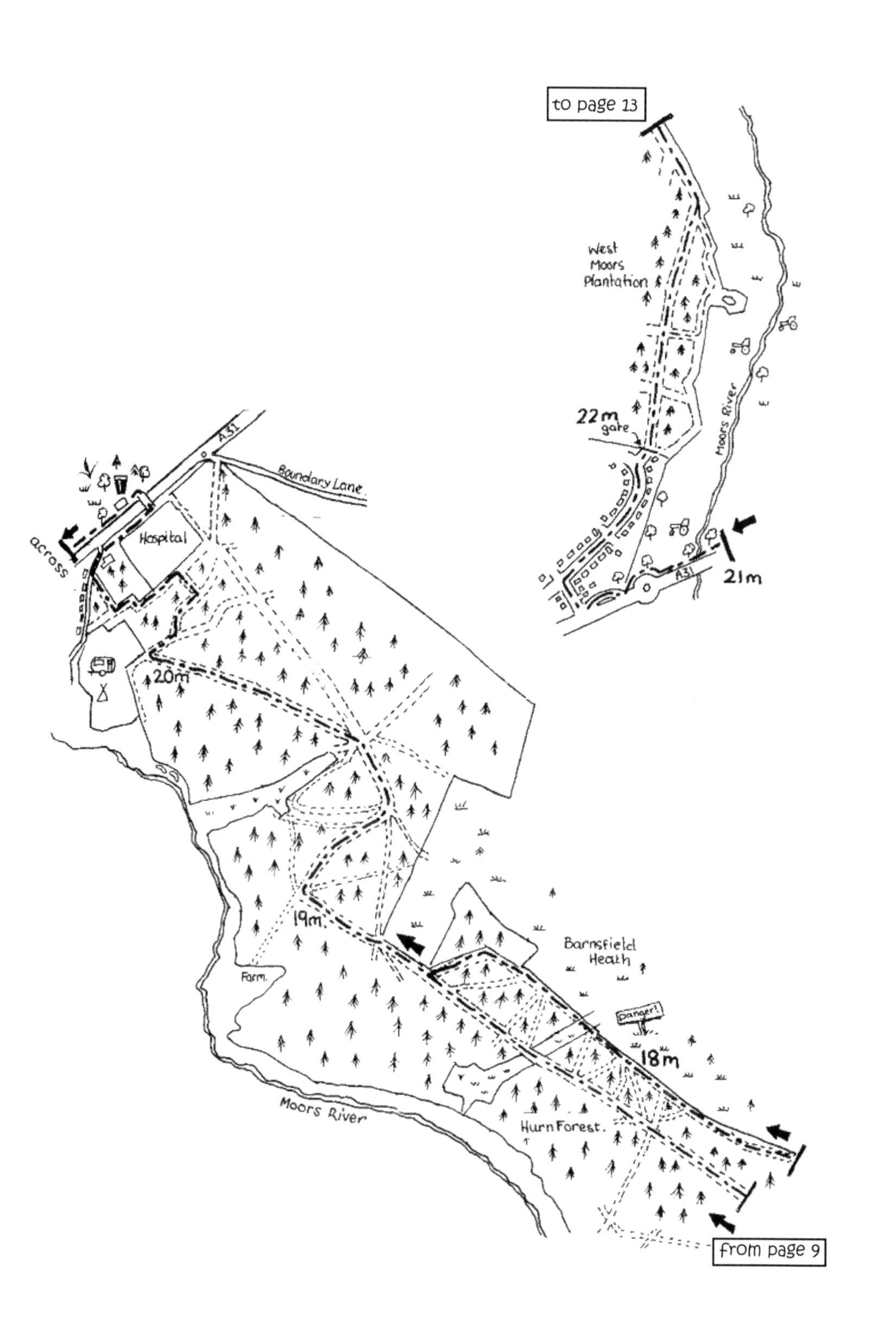

to page 13
West
Moors
Plantation
22m
gate
Moors River
21m
A31
Boundary Lane
Hospital
across
20m
19m
Farm.
Barnsfield
Heath
Danger!
18m
Moors River
Hurn Forest.
from page 9

Continue along the forest track until it makes a clear turn to the southwest with a belt of cleared ground to its right

At this point, a track continues ahead to meet the dismantled railway at a wooden bar gate. Take this and turn right to head along the old line (north east). You will soon cross an old steel railway bridge across the River Moors. Lions Hill is a wooded hump on the right set in heathland. Anyone who has obtained accommodation at the 'Little Lion's Farm' will find a private track on the left that saves a mile from the route. All others must carry on until the backs of houses are passed and a footpath is reached on the left, into a pleasant sub-urban road {Forest Edge Drive – see drawing overleaf} This shortly emerges on to the busy Horton Road opposite the entrance to West Moors Country Park. Turn left and make your way along this for ¾ mile.

The Wooden bar-gate on to the dismantled railway West Moors Plantation.

disused railway bridge over the Moors River.

After passing a campsite (Woolsbridge Manor Farm) start to look on the right for a gateway festooned with signs to an industrial estate. Before heading up here, a visit to the nearby pub may be worthwhile. (The Old Barn Farm.)

The bridle path commences as a metalled surface that begins to break up as we pass to the left of the industrial units. There a gateway of leaping horses and cartwheels seems somewhat incongruous. This track becomes increasingly less used. The views soon become more expansive and will draw you on towards Verwood in the north. A line of trees on your right serves as a guide rail with no obvious turnings other than one small path off to the right to the 'West Moors Country Park'. All is peaceful here apart from the odd 'toot' from the model railway and the sound of golfers hidden behind the trees.

After passing an area of wetter ground to the left (Rushmore Pond), the path becomes a single one and narrows as it enters a wood. The way through the wood is clear, though wet at times. As the trees thin, a pylon is passed by at very close quarters. Twenty yards on, at a crossing of narrow cart tracks, go to the left and follow the path as it then turns right alongside the new, but rather grand, Potterne Farm Cottage.

Playing fields and play area appear on the right. Turn towards this and walk around the changing rooms etc, to pick up the path, quarter left, across the fields. The path crosses the stream that hitherto we have called The Moors, but from now on we will have to call the Crane. (A small, but important feature of our route and the land through which it passes, lending its name, as it does, to Cranborne Chase).

The path becomes tarmac as it enters a housing estate and there ceases to resemble a bridleway. One imagines the only bridles it sees are attached to toddlers rather than horses. Keep on this path as it crosses suburban roads. Across a cul-de-sac, take the gravel path and cross the next road to the unmade 'Moneyfly Road'. This ends at a junction with the B3081.

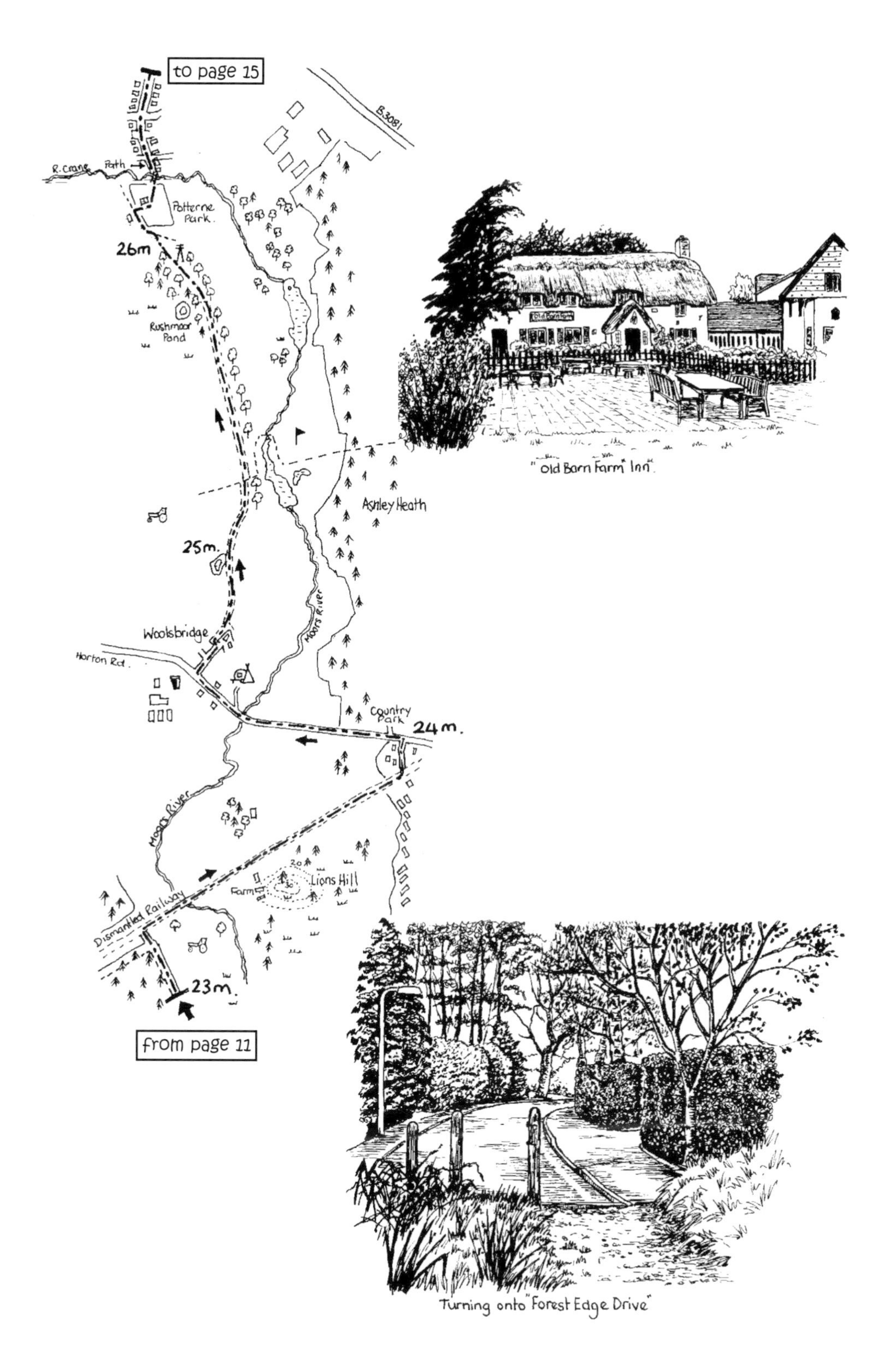

"Old Barn Farm" Inn.

Turning onto "Forest Edge Drive"

Verwood to Cranborne (5 miles)

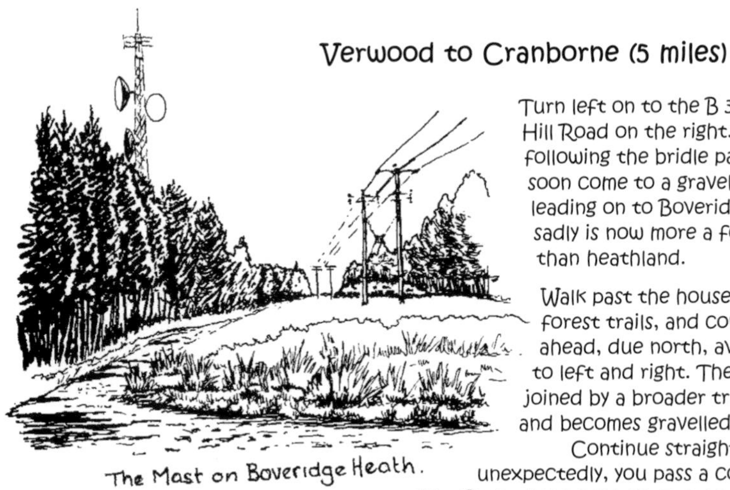
The Mast on Boveridge Heath.

Turn left on to the B 3081 as far as Noon Hill Road on the right. Walk up here following the bridle path sign. You will soon come to a gravel track ahead, leading on to Boveridge Heath, which sadly is now more a forest plantation than heathland.

Walk past the houses to a junction of forest trails, and continue straight-ahead, due north, avoiding all tracks to left and right. The track is soon joined by a broader trail from the right and becomes gravelled.

Continue straight ahead until, unexpectedly, you pass a cottage on the right. Beyond the cottage turn to the left. Our route continues to gain height until a communications mast appears on the right. Turn towards this and then go to the left through a bar gate to continue on a main track to the northwest for ½ mile.

Ignore both tempting paths that lie off the main track, but after the track curves left and is met by a wooden bar, take the path to the right. This is a narrower, less established path that soon begins to descend from Pistle Hill. The forest changes character as we descend, with more far-reaching glimpses to the right. Towards the bottom of the hill the path meets a track from the right and passes a small campsite (Hillside). A little further on and we cross what appears to be an old railway bridge.

Gotham Farm, Entrance Driveway

When you reach a tarmac road, a choice is available. Either go ahead for ¼ mile until a bridle path is met alongside the Heavy Horse Centre, or to turn right and explore the area around Gotham Farm. This is less straightforward but has more interest and is the route I will describe.

On the bend in the road, turn left into Gotham Farm. Pass through the main gate ahead and walk through the farm itself, passing between the farm buildings. Through the farmyard, the right of way turns to the left and, taking care not to disturb its equestrian residents, pass through a second gate. Immediately through the gate a footpath crosses a field on the right to the far corner. There is no stile, only a metal gate, and the path itself is invisible, but a stile in the far corner allows the route to be followed on the same course across the next field. Don't head for the far corner, but descend to the right before the corner is reached to a little used and hidden stile. (A pylon in the field beyond the trees provides a useful marker). The stile gives access to a lovely bluebell wood. Descend half left to a stream and wooden plank bridge. Cross this and ascend steeply (¾ left) across an open and possibly overgrown area to a small gap in a hedgerow (A stick to beat down the bracken etc may be useful). Cross the next field half left or skirt it to the left, to a stile that brings you down on to a narrow path (Purbeck Lane).

Over the stile, descend initially to the left, and then turn right on to a clear bridle path (the one you would have been on had you decided on the alternative that went past the (Heavy Horse Centre).

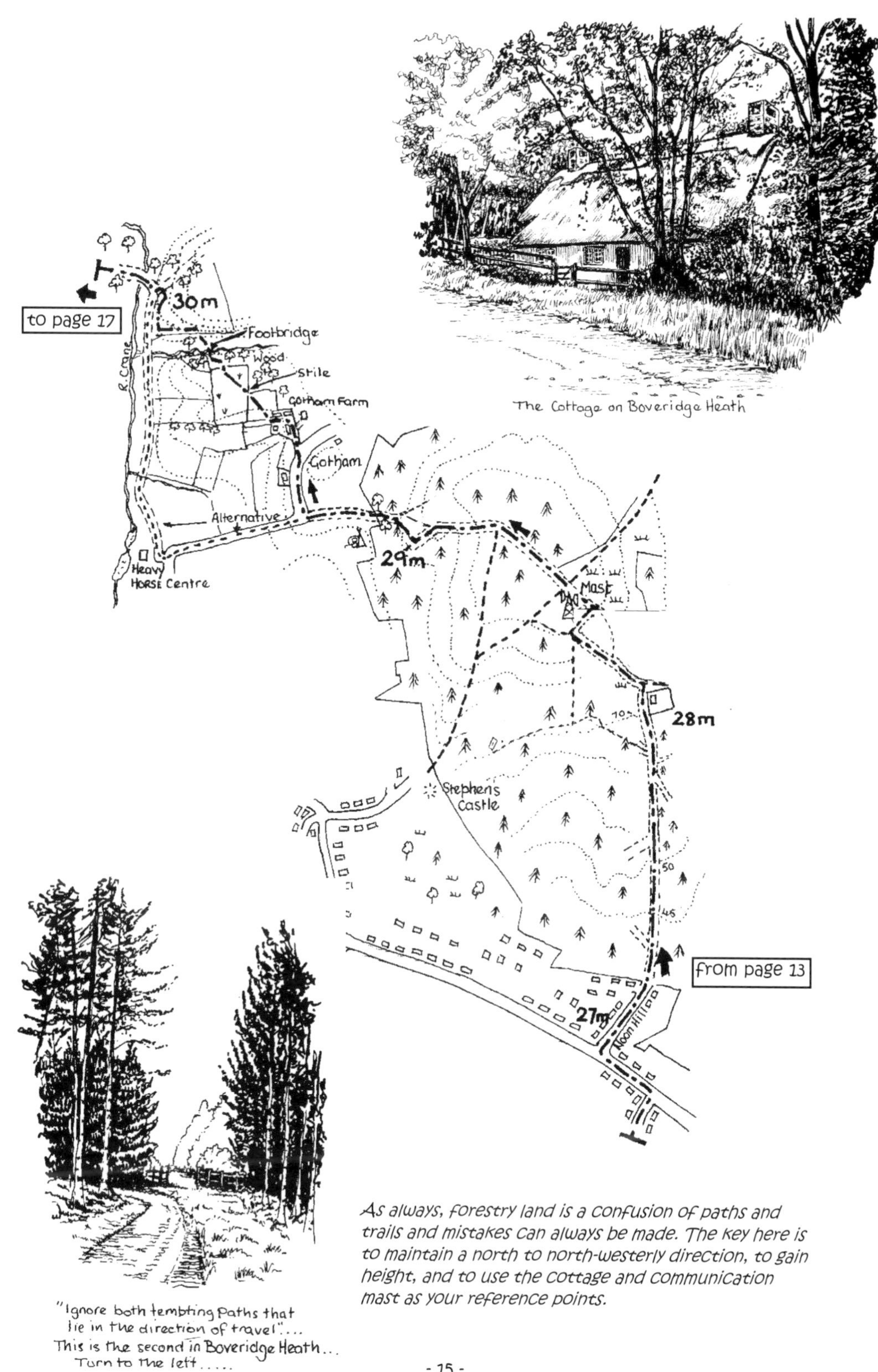

The Cottage on Boveridge Heath

"Ignore both tempting paths that lie in the direction of travel"... This is the second in Boveridge Heath... Turn to the left.....

As always, forestry land is a confusion of paths and trails and mistakes can always be made. The key here is to maintain a north to north-westerly direction, to gain height, and to use the cottage and communication mast as your reference points.

The route ahead on the bridle path is clear and crosses the Crane at an old sluice gate as it continues through woodland, rounds Great Rhymes Copse, and passes alongside Castle Hill Woods. Walking is easy and the scenery is restful on the senses. In spring, bluebells and primroses carpet these woods and wild garlic scents the verges. Through the trees to the right, wider views across Cranborne Chase become more frequent, promoting a sense of anticipation. Two tracks join it from the right, but ignore them and instead follow this ancient lane for nearly 1½ miles.

Towards the end of the lane the ground on the left begins to rise in tree-covered banks or terraces as Castle Hill is approached. Look for a stile among the trees lining the right hand side of the path (See drawing overleaf). It leads away from the wood towards Cranborne, half left across a field. Go down to the far corner and across a second stile. Go first to the right and then immediately left on to the suburban road into the centre of the village. The road arrives at a junction alongside the Cranborne Chase Information Centre and the Fleur de Lys Pub, opposite the church. At the corner turn right into the village and then left on the Boveridge Road to the square, and the Sheaf of Arrows.

Cranborne.

Having refreshed oneself, I assume, continue on the Boveridge Road and as it makes a turn to the right, way markers on the left between houses, point the way on to the Jubilee Trail which we will follow for a while.

The way ahead is clear, first rising through a park-like area with the possible company of black-fleeced sheep. At a gate and farm buildings we join a tarmac farm road from the left, continue ahead for a ½ mile past farmland, alongside the infant River Crane, under the gaze of the resident 'long horned cattle'.

At Cranborne Farm the track becomes less formal and, turning to the right, rises to a ridge at Jack's Hedge Corner and a rewarding view ahead. Turn to the left and head northwest towards the high ground of Pentridge Hill. This is a wonderful stretch culminating with the Pentridge ridge itself and should be savoured. This is Cranborne Chase at its most picturesque so take every opportunity to turn and look around.

Jack's Hedge Corner.

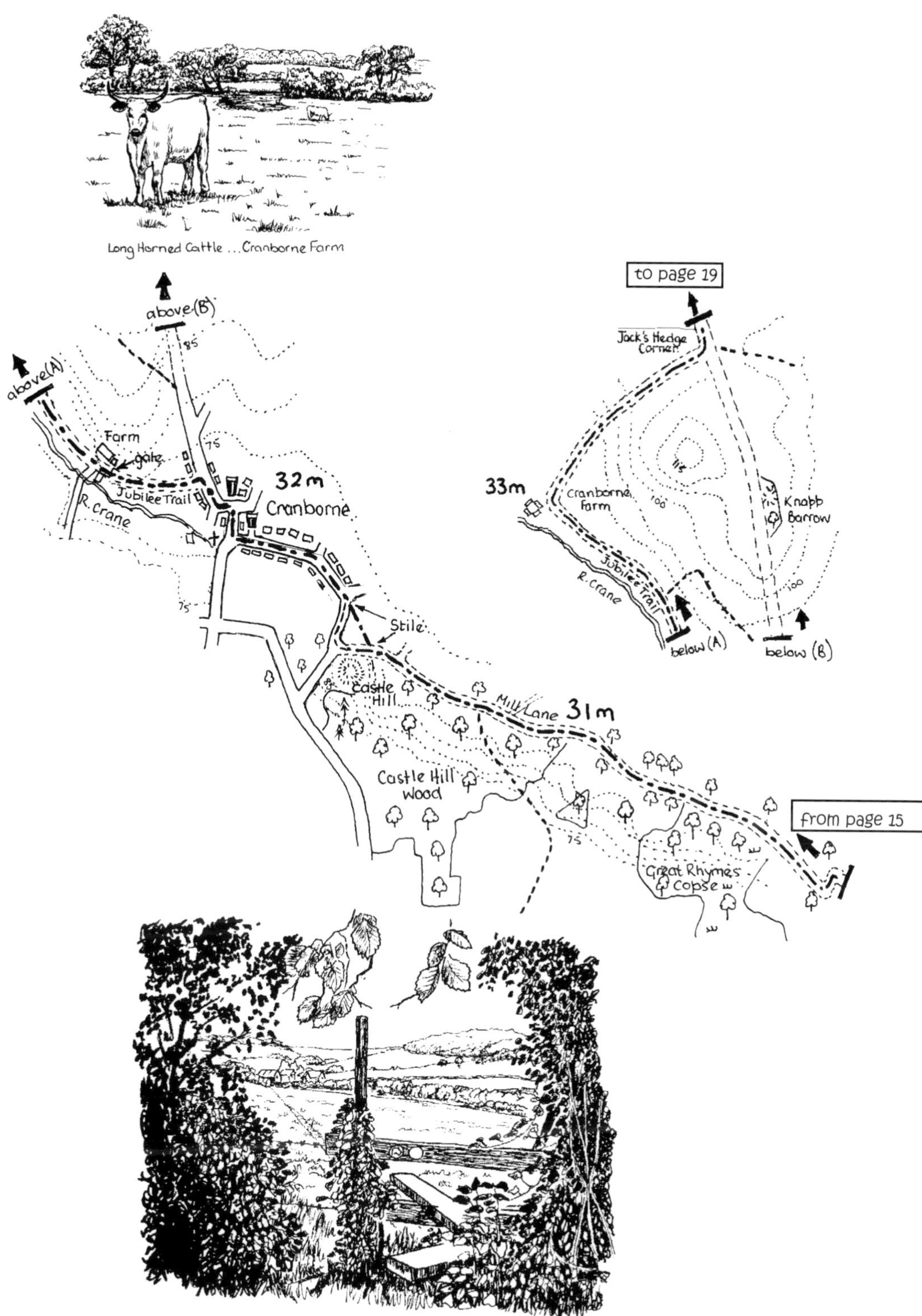

Long Horned Cattle ... Cranborne Farm

Leaving the path below Castle Hill into Cranborne

Cranborne to Sixpenny Handley (7 miles)

With Pentridge Hill ahead, and retrospective views of the Chase, the track first descends then rises up to the ridge ahead with a high hawthorn hedge to the right. As this hedge ends, the fields to the right become almost park-like and seem to be the home of a large number of hares.

North-West from Pentridge Hill.

Passing through a metal gate, the way remains clearly marked and gives a choice to the left or half right. The left offers a short cut by-passing the village of Pentridge. If time or energy is short this is an option but it misses a wonderful 1 mile loop along the ridge and around Penbury Knoll, the site of an Iron-age hill fort. Instead then, turn to the right and walk, on a grassy track, alongside stunted trees and to the left of a fence, enjoying as you do the extensive views west towards Sixpenny Handley and beyond.

This is a first rate spot to rest in the afternoon sun and anticipate the route ahead. A gate to its right enters the wooded Penbury Knoll. To the left of the track, the ground rises beneath a canopy of trees, on grass, to an old trig point. There is an enchantment to this place and a sense of peace that will encourage you to stay awhile.

Beyond the tree line, descend immediately to the left down a steep bank alongside gorse bushes and a marshy pond, to a stile ahead, and into a field. Across the stile, turn left and follow the fence line back around the knoll on rising ground. At its gentle summit ridge descend to the right on an indistinct path, to a fence. Continue to descend alongside the fence, across a stile and down a narrow path between hedges. At the bottom the path emerges in a drive. Half right is a gate on to the road through Pentridge.

"St Rumbold's" Pentridge.

The church is worth a visit, otherwise turn to the left. As the road turns to the right, continue ahead on a much-used farm track. Towards its end, turn with it to the right, following the footpath signs, on a slight ascent into a field system. At the second gate, the O.S. map indicates a path moving slightly west (½ left). This remarkable right of way crosses two ancient landmarks as it rises onto the open field and then descends to the A354. It first moves away from the fence crossing the Dorset Cursus before turning back to the right beyond the summit of the field. The right of way descends to cross the path of Ackling Dyke, the Roman road that once linked London to Exeter. The original road and bank, built in the first century, remain clear at this point as they come alongside the busy A354 that takes up this more ancient of routes. At the A354, a garage offers food and some refreshment.

Cross the road with care, and continue on the track ahead to the left of a private dwelling, and follow it as it turns west along the field boundary on a green path across Oakley Down. After a little under a mile, cross a metalled farm road alongside a bungalow and continue down the field ahead. To the left a long barrow, Wor Barrow, is more evidence of ancient occupation. Sixpenny Handley, its church and campsite, are now seen ahead.

At a junction of paths continue on towards the church. Cross a minor road, and once over a stile, cross a field until a left turn, away from the church, leads you into a narrow hedge lined track, to emerge alongside the Post Office and pub/general store. (continues p.19)

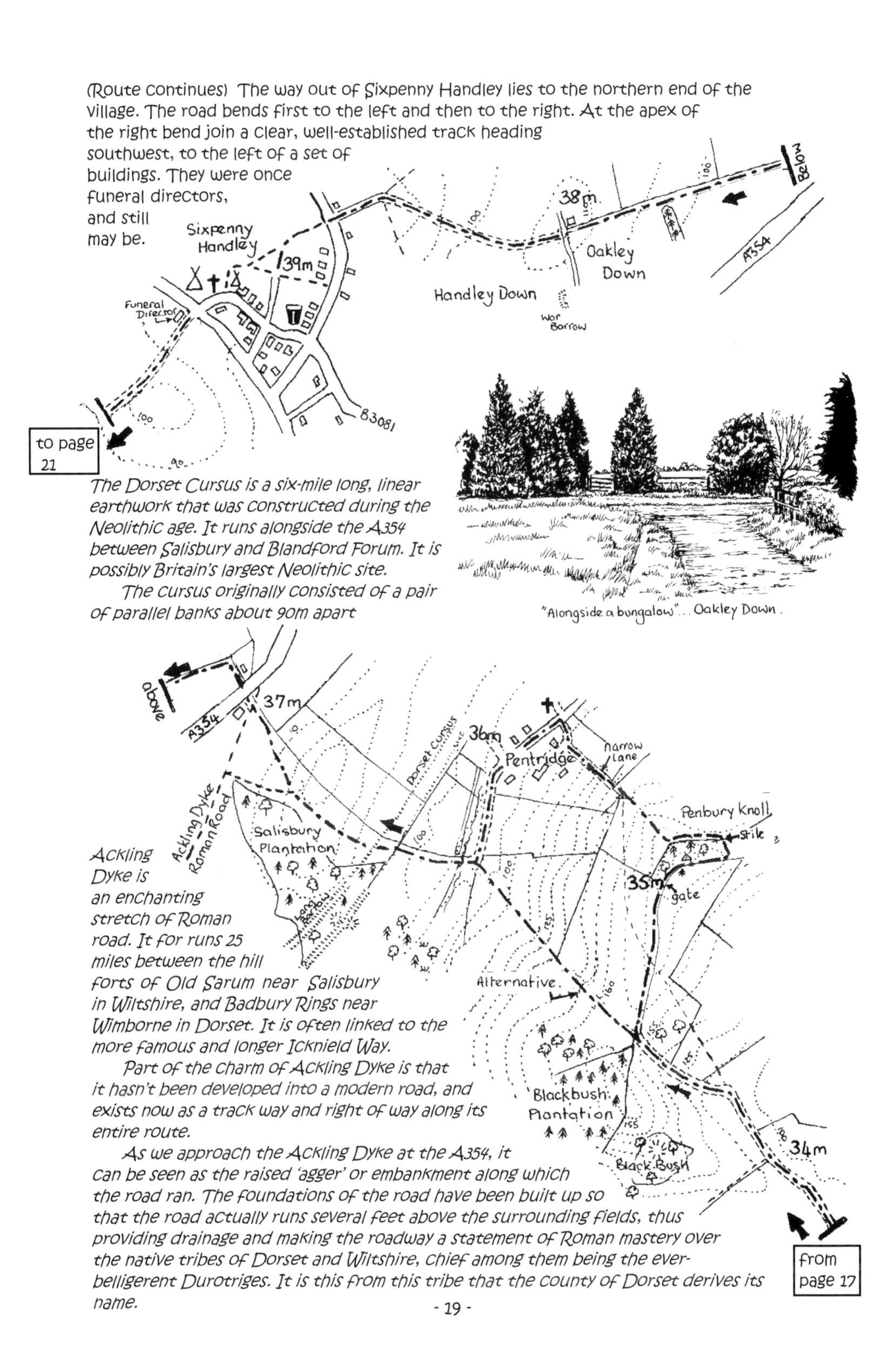

(Route continues) The way out of Sixpenny Handley lies to the northern end of the village. The road bends first to the left and then to the right. At the apex of the right bend join a clear, well-established track heading southwest, to the left of a set of buildings. They were once funeral directors, and still may be.

to page 21

The Dorset Cursus is a six-mile long, linear earthwork that was constructed during the Neolithic age. It runs alongside the A354 between Salisbury and Blandford Forum. It is possibly Britain's largest Neolithic site.

The cursus originally consisted of a pair of parallel banks about 90m apart

Ackling Dyke is an enchanting stretch of Roman road. It for runs 25 miles between the hill forts of Old Sarum near Salisbury in Wiltshire, and Badbury Rings near Wimborne in Dorset. It is often linked to the more famous and longer Icknield Way.

Part of the charm of Ackling Dyke is that it hasn't been developed into a modern road, and exists now as a track way and right of way along its entire route.

As we approach the Ackling Dyke at the A354, it can be seen as the raised 'agger' or embankment along which the road ran. The foundations of the road have been built up so that the road actually runs several feet above the surrounding fields, thus providing drainage and making the roadway a statement of Roman mastery over the native tribes of Dorset and Wiltshire, chief among them being the ever-belligerent Durotriges. It is this from this tribe that the county of Dorset derives its name.

from page 17

Sixpenny Handley – Shaftesbury (18 miles)

Approaching Dean.

The track from Sixpenny Handley remains clear and well established for ½ mile. As it passes a collection of buildings on the left, to the accompaniment of the barking of large dogs, the track becomes less well used. When a gate ahead is reached, take an even less well used track to the left which continues in a south westerly direction for a further ½ mile or so. On the way the path meets the Jubilee Way once more at a bend in a tarmac road. Continue straight ahead to the hamlet of Dean alongside a cottage.

Cross the road ahead to a field gate and walk alongside the fence until, after less than 200 yards, a small stile on the right breaches the fence into another field. The path, which at the time of writing was not clear, crosses the field on a left diagonal to the far corner where a broken stile leads on to a narrow, tree-lined track (named the Straight Lane on the OS map). Turn to the left and begin the descent into Minchington. Through a metal gate continue ahead until, after a ¼ mile, the track meets a farm track with a gate opposite. On the gate there are obscure signs declaring the existence of a bridleway in times of flooding. Assuming this not to be the case, turn right and follow the farm track to a gate. In the absence of a stile, climb over to the road and turn left.

When the road makes a turn to the left, go through a gate on the right alongside a house. It feels, for all the world, as though you are trespassing, but carry on alongside the garden and through a copse, alongside a ditch to a second gate leading into a field. A clear path crosses it on a diagonal to the right towards an electrical sub-station and a tarmac road.

Cross the road to a stile in the hedgerow and a right of way that descends ¼ right across the first field, then alongside another, to a stile in the next corner and so to a path alongside a cottage. At the road, turn right, towards the village

Farnham is an attractive little village, but with the exception of the Museum Inn, lacks opportunities for rest and refreshment. The pub itself offers rather superior food and one gets the impression a mud spattered, warm and weary walker might feel a little out of place. Do not be put off and feel you have to remain outside with other 'less desirables', leave your boots outside and enjoy a glass of good ale.

The Museum Inn, Farnham.

(The Museum Inn was extended and renamed to accommodate visitors to a nearby museum. The renowned archaeologist General Pitt Rivers, established the museum in the late 19th century to exhibit finds from the Romano- British village at Rushmore. The museum no longer exists but much of the collection can still be seen in museums in Salisbury and Oxford.)

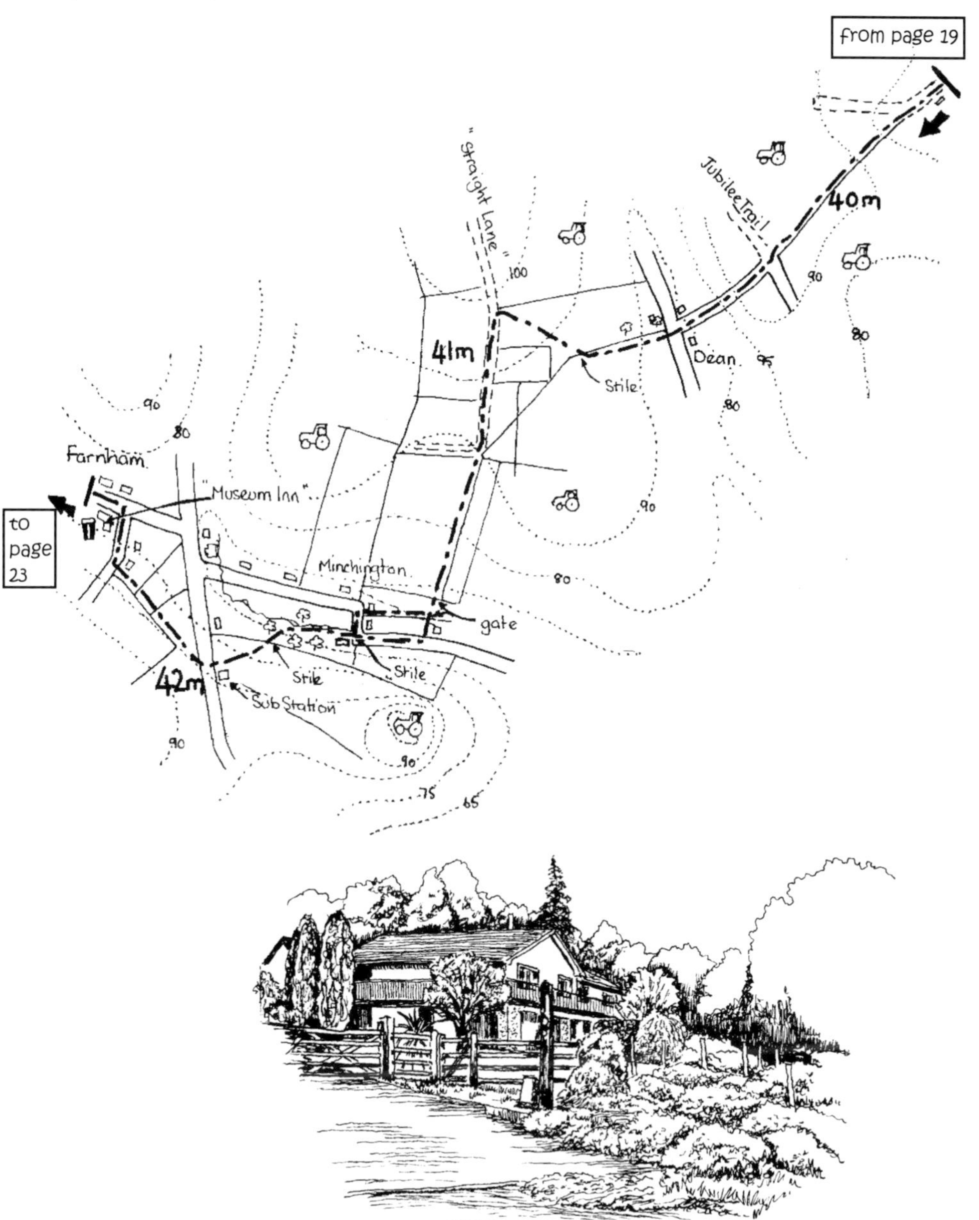

The footpath gate in Minchington

Take your leave of Farnham by heading up the village past the pub on the left. When footpath signs to right and left are reached, turn left alongside what appears to be a chapel or church hall. The path continues to the right of the building to open on to a field, without an obvious path across it. Head west (½ right) towards the far right corner as best you can. The path emerges on to a minor road alongside a cottage.

Turn right, until in a short while the road bends to the right. Here, turn left down a metalled track towards the well-appointed Hookswood House. The right of way continues past the house as a green path between a wire fence and trees (glimpses through the trees provide a sight of well-tended gardens). The path narrows to a single track, which may be

'New Barn' Chettle Common.

muddy in wet weather, and passes a hedge to emerge into a field with refreshingly expansive views across open country. With larks singing, turn to the right alongside a broken fence (250°) until a short wooden fence obstructs the way. It shepherds you left, down the field, on a wide green path.

At the bottom of the field, before the trees, turn right alongside the field hedge heading towards a wooded area (Chettle Common). The OS map indicates the presence of ancient settlements that are not immediately apparent. (If at this stage you happen to find a propelling pencil, please return it to the author – Thank you.)

At the end of the field the feet are drawn on, along an attractive ride alongside the coppice to the right, but our route heads south (left), towards a metal farm building (New Barn) where a clear farm track is met. Continue ahead to cross the track and to follow a right of way (Jubilee Way) alongside a field. Through the gate in the next corner, turn right to follow the next field edge around the corner of the field to a stile on the right. Cross the stile and turn to the left and walk around the field in a clockwise direction to meet a tarmac farm road from the right.

Continue ahead along a green path (A drove in the old Dorset dialect) that, in 200 yards, makes a turn to the left to cross a stile.

The surroundings now change profoundly from agriculture to the once opulent environs of Eastbury Park. Once over the stile, turn to the right (southwest.) and enjoy a walk along an avenue of trees towards a gated coppice. The path then leads around the rear gardens of cottages and into the village of Tarrant Gunville.

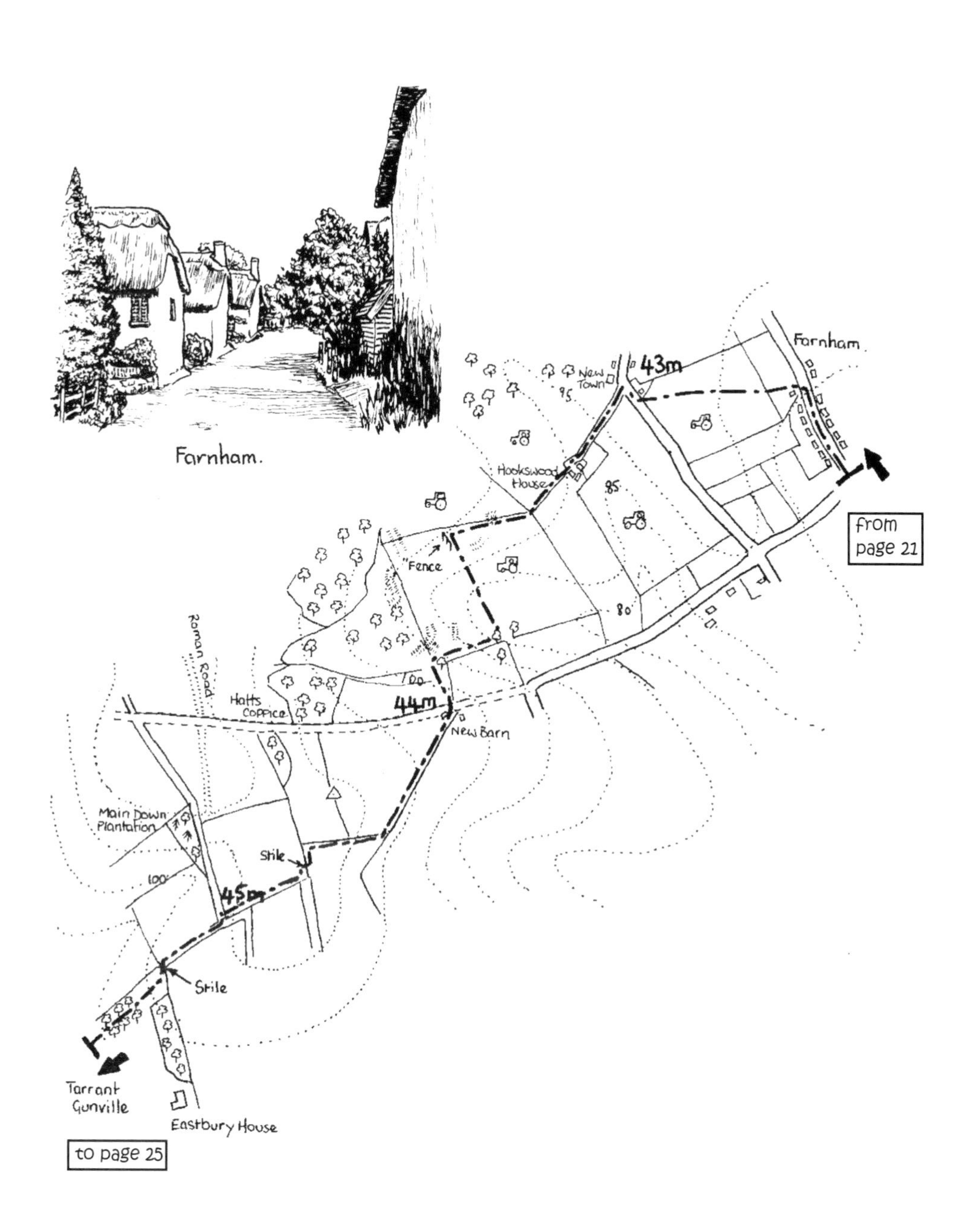

Eastbury House once claimed to be the largest and finest country mansion in Dorset. It was completed in 1738 for George Bubb Dodington. On the death of the original owners however, with no new owner forthcoming, three quarters of it was demolished in the 1770s and 80s. Only the stable block, converted into a house, now remains. At one time this was owned by no less a luminary than Josiah Wedgewood. It is suggested that a resident spook is numbered among its current occupants.

Like so many of the villages in this part of North Dorset, Tarrant Gunville offers little for the walker, there are no shops and the pub has long since stopped providing travellers with refreshment. So, having turned right along the road, turn immediately left up the hill alongside the church until a fingerboard indicates a stile and footpath on the right. (Some refreshment may be found, a half-mile further up this road, at a Farm shop.)

The right of way, beyond the stile, makes its way behind cottages and along the bottom of fields using a further succession of stiles. The footpath passes disused farm buildings and 'sewage plant' to a stile. From here it skirts a field on a narrow path initially alongside cottages to arrive at a stile and a collection of cottages (In the summer months this section of the path can become poorly maintained and may necessitate retreating to the road for a few hundred yards in order to by-pass the field.)

Behind the cottages, and accompanying buildings, the path continues parallel to the road and shortly after passes through a gate into a more open meadow. As the gradient from the left steepens, remain on the same contour and head for a corner in the wooded area to a stile that gives access to a path, through the trees, skirting above cottage gardens. This path meets its end at a stile as it emerges from the copse and joins the road from Tarrant Gunville. Go down to the road, over another stile and turn right.

On to the track towards Hanging Coppice.

On the bend of the road, make a left turn onto a track, alongside sheep pens and along the bottom of a steepening valley. (The homeowner of the cottage on the left at this point seems to have a keen interest in golf)

As the ground rises the valley sides draw in and views are lost as Hanging Coppice is entered. The path here is well used by horses and may be heavy going in wet weather. There is also plenty of evidence here of a large population of pheasants, specifically the spent cartridge shells that persecuted them. The coppice is an attractive place with primroses and assorted flora making the going pleasant.

At the end of the coppice, we arrive at an intersection of ways. The path on the left comes from Iwerne Minster and Iwerne Courtney and straight ahead plunges into the depths of Ashmore Wood. Our way is more indistinct but to the right (north-east), on rising ground alongside a fence and the forest edge, along the Wessex Ridgeway.

All forest tracks from the left are passed by until way markers are encountered at the summit of the second rise. An effort has been made to give character to the fingerposts. In spite of their tendency to point upwards, turn to the left towards Ashmore and away from the forest edge into the wood itself.

On emerging from the wood a ¼ mile further on, the track remains northerly and clear as it rises along 'Halfpenny Lane' to the Village of Ashmore ½ mile ahead.

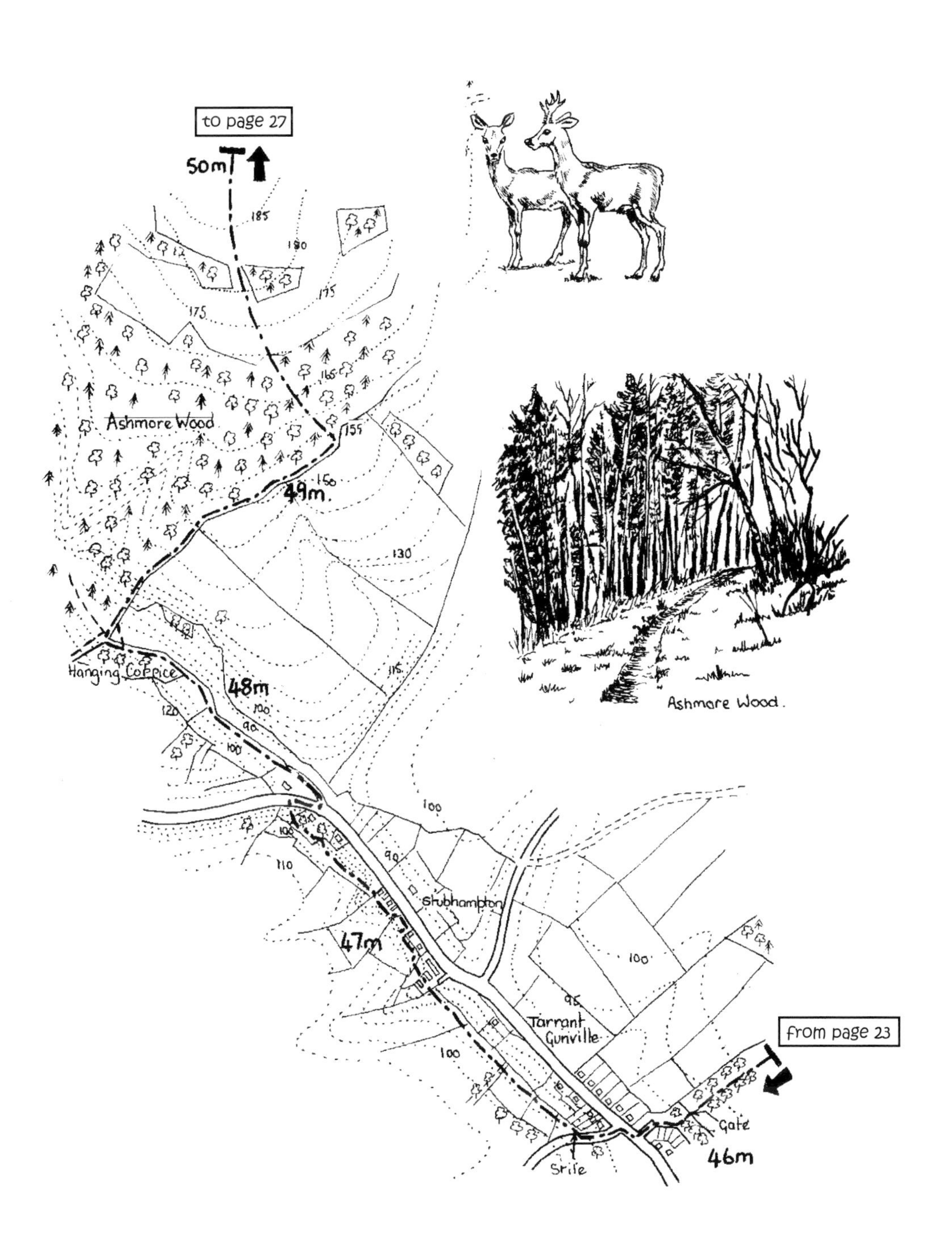
to page 27
50m
185
180
175
175
165
155
Ashmore Wood
150
49m.
130
115
Hanging Coppice
48m
120
100
90
100
100
100
90
110
Stubhampton
47m
100
95
Tarrant Gunville
100
from page 23
Gate
46m
Stile
Ashmore Wood.

All Ashmore can offer the weary traveller is the church and a duck pond, so having explored these, go to the west for 100 yards along the road past the church, then Manor Farm and its buildings.

At a gate on the right, a little used grassy path, between fields, (a drove) reveals our route towards Shepherd's Bottom. After about a ¼ mile, with the steep valley before you, turn right through a gate along the top of the field.

At the end of the field, descend to the left along the fence line. The track becomes clearer during the course of the descent and through a gate at the bottom becomes more used. Once past a wooded area on your left, take the choice of ways that climbs steeply, half left, towards the higher ground. Shepherds Bottom is a sheltered and peaceful spot and grows more attractive as we climb away from it.

Shepherd's Bottom.

As the climb eases, pass through a gate. Our route then makes a turn to the right along the fence-line. Continue on this bearing (350°) and head through another gate, alongside a hedgerow, towards West Wood. A gate ahead enters the wood. Ignoring all other tracks, carry on through the wood alongside its perimeter fence. West Wood has an ancient feel to it and this is especially so when a valley, descending left, is passed. Robin Hood would feel at home here.

As the path ahead begins to rise, the sound of traffic gives warning of the road alongside Compton Abbas Airfield, which is soon reached. Cross it to a stile in the hedgerow ahead. Another stile 15 yards to the left gives access to the airfield. Notices warn of the dangers of low flying aircraft and the rules for safe conduct, but it seems to me that the first ought to be 'keep your head down'. (If the crossing of the airfield seems too daunting, instead continue left along the road past the flying club. Cross the road at a junction and climb the stile, there turn right along the footpath that runs alongside the road as far as the access gate to Compton Down shown below).

The route across the airfield is on a diagonal to the left, towards a double stile in the hedgerow ahead. Once over the stile, turn to the left to skirt the top of the field to a gap in the corner at the top of Spread Eagle Hill.

All along here your attention will be held by the wonderful views to the north across Melbury Down, the little hamlet and church in Melbury Abbas, and to the northwest, the high ground of Melbury Hill. It is a walk to be relished if a little uneven under foot. This minor flaw is soon to be remedied.

Cross the road above Spread Eagle Hill with care, to a 'pull-in' and a gate that gives access to National Trust land. Here is walking par-excellence on grass, across Compton Down. The route continues to follow the fence on your left towards Melbury Beacon.

Access Gate to Compton Down and Melbury Hill.

The flying club at Compton Abbas Airfield, when open, offers the attraction of excellent food and refreshment at its café and bar. It is certainly worth a diversion.

Compton Abbas Airfield. The perimeter fence and stile.

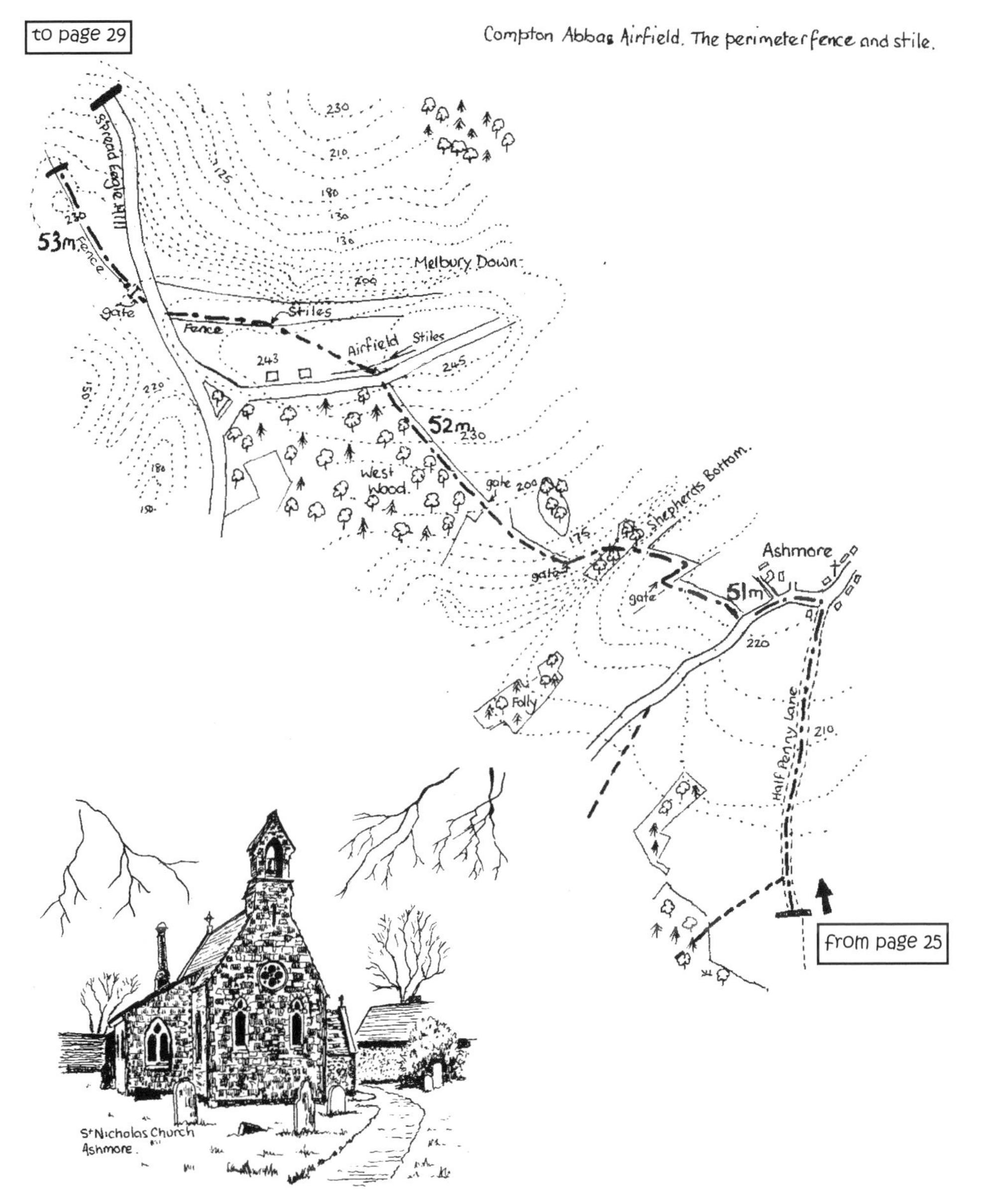

After a steep descent, the ground soon rises again past the earthworks of Cross Dykes, and through a gate in an electric fence. (A fence that may, or may not be there!) The summit of the Beacon, across a fence on the left, is marked by a trig point (SB041), which is now converted into a 'sighting table' for the area. Cross the stile to it, and survey the land around you. It provides an insight into the route ahead.

The path from The Beacon is not very clear but heads slightly northwest (353°) towards Shaftesbury, on the ridge ahead, with the tower of Holy Trinity Church prominent on the skyline. The path soon steepens and crosses a ditch of an earthwork on the way. Across a stile, the route descends to pass through two kissing gates to the roadway. Turn immediately right, alongside a row of houses.

A third of mile on and as the road begins to descend farm buildings are passed on the left. Shortly afterwards take a footpath, on the left, via a stile beneath a tree. The path (not clear), goes down the field angling away from the fence to the far corner. A double stile crosses a watercourse and boggy ground towards the busy A350 and an odd construction that turns out to be boulders in a steel framework buttressing the road behind it. At the road, turn right towards Cann. (A river flows rapidly into the ponds on the left). Shortly after, turn left on to a metalled track towards Cann Mills. Past the millpond and the windmill turn right through a gate in front of the house ahead. Continue alongside the house, across a small field/pasture.

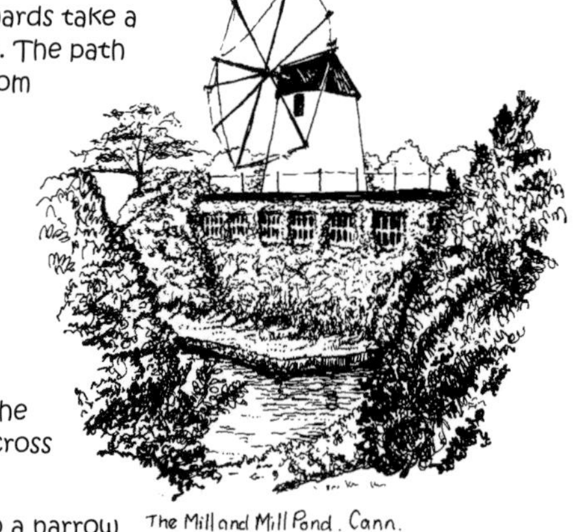
The Mill and Mill Pond. Cann.

Go over the stile in the corner of the field into a narrow pasture. Keeping to the left, in a very short while, search for a small footbridge across a stream into a muddy field. Go to the right along the field edge to a stile in the next corner.

Continue along the field bottom. With higher ground on the left, continue on amidst scenes of pastoral calm through a series of stiles to finally emerge on the narrowest of country roads. (French Mill Lane). Turn right to head north past the mill itself. The road soon rises ahead on its way towards Shaftesbury.

At a junction, (Three Ways) take the narrower road to the right and continue upwards for around ¾ mile to the second stile in the bank on the right. The stile leads into the area known as the 'Wilderness'. This provides an excellent way into Shaftesbury first across a field, through a gate, and then on a green path alongside a woodland area that appears to have real age. The town looms ever nearer, both ahead and across the valley to the left.

Gold Hill. Shaftesbury.

At a kissing gate that opens to a small road, turn left to descend to a junction. Turn left back on to French Mill Lane and, shortly after, turn down a footpath to the right alongside a post box. This first evolves into a wider track and then into a metalled surface alongside homes with wonderful views. At main junction, turn right (St James Street) and begin to hum the largo from the 'New World Symphony' for shortly you will be ascending Gold Hill, made famous by the Hovis advert. Turn left up the hill.

Gold Hill comes to an abrupt halt at its summit with a gift shop and cafe that, though welcome, is something of a disappointment. But turn and look behind you. This little hill remains a charming snapshot of the past and more than justifies its place on countless chocolate boxes. You have just entered Shaftesbury by the finest possible route.

The building that constitutes the barrier at the summit of Gold Hill turns out to be the rear of the old Town Hall. Alleyways to the left or right (past the museum and St Peter's Church) spill out on to the High Street and here can be found refreshment in plenty. Shaftesbury is an obvious place for 'R & R', not least because of its significance to the ARD walker, it being the furthest point north we shall go. It's all downhill from here!

B and Bs abound, and if permission is sought in advance, camping can be arranged at the grounds of Shaftesbury Football Club in Coppice Street.

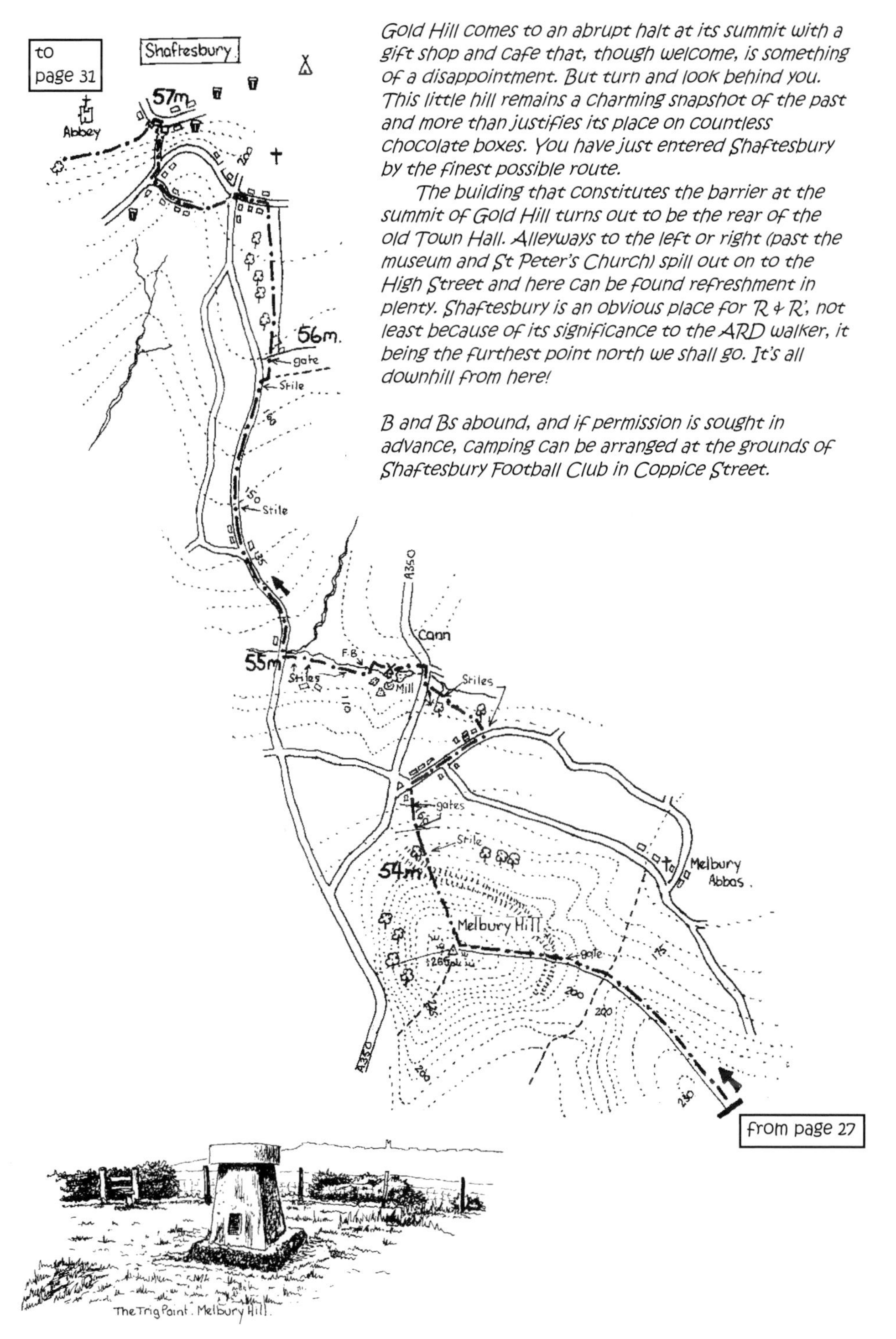

The Trig Point. Melbury Hill.

Holy Trinity Church Shaftesbury.

Gold Hill to Marnhull (8 miles)

Having taken a well earned rest and recharged the rucksack; the walk is resumed from in front of the Town Hall. From here, turn to the west (left) to walk along the scenic Park Walk with wonderful views back across Melbury Hill and the South. This path takes you past the gateway to the Abbey Museum and the Holy Trinity Church and on towards a choice of narrower pathways ahead. Take the right hand one (Pine Walk) to its end on St John's Hill, and turn left to descend toward St James Church at its base. Here turn first right on to Foyle Hill Road.

With signposts to Marnhull, the road continues with a real sense that Shaftesbury is already far behind. The feeling that 'it is all downhill from Shaftesbury' can only be encouraged on this first section of the walk.

In around ½ mile, Edwards Farm is passed, (Now the surgery of a osteopath). Shortly after, at a junction of roads, pass a turning on the left and then, at a fork in the road, turn to the left signposted to Marnhull (4 miles).

After ½ mile, just beyond Thomas' Farm, a half hidden fingerboard on the right indicates the path towards Duncliffe Hill and Jade Wood Farm, along a clear farm track. (Blynfield Farm, passed a little before Thomas' Farm, is now more like an industrial site or storage area).

The track soon deteriorates and, beyond a bungalow, takes a turn to the left. The track ends at a gate. Many paths cross the hill and some can even avoid the climb to the summit, but the preferred route turns right, once through the gate, to continue along the hedgerow. As the hedgerow makes a turn to the right, a gate ahead gives access to woodland and Duncliffe Hill.

The path begins by turning right but soon turns again to the west and climbs, increasingly steeply, to the summit. (Avoid all sidetracks during both the ascent and descent.) Duncliffe is maintained by The Woodland Trust and the Friends of Duncliffe and, thanks to their efforts, remains a lovely bluebell wood in the spring, and a delight to walk at all times.

Towards the summit glimpses to the North open up and, after a couple of false summits, we arrive at the short summit ridge and trig point. The descent, when it comes, is abrupt. At a gate at the bottom of the hill, a choice of routes is on offer, one continuing around the base of the hill remaining in the wood. However, the official route leaves the woodland, using the stile into the field ahead. Follow the fence-line to the corner of the field and turn to the left to follow alongside the woodland and across two fields until you meet a main track into the wood. Turn to the right and walk away from the wood to the road 150 yards ahead.

At the road turn to the right for twenty yards then turn left into the lane alongside a corner cottage. Continue along the lane for a ½ mile and just beyond Chequer's Farm. Turn to the left into 'Angel Lane'.

Duncliffe Wood seen from alongside "Lanzerac House". Near 'Alcester' on the road from Shaftesbury.

Park Walk. Shaftesbury.

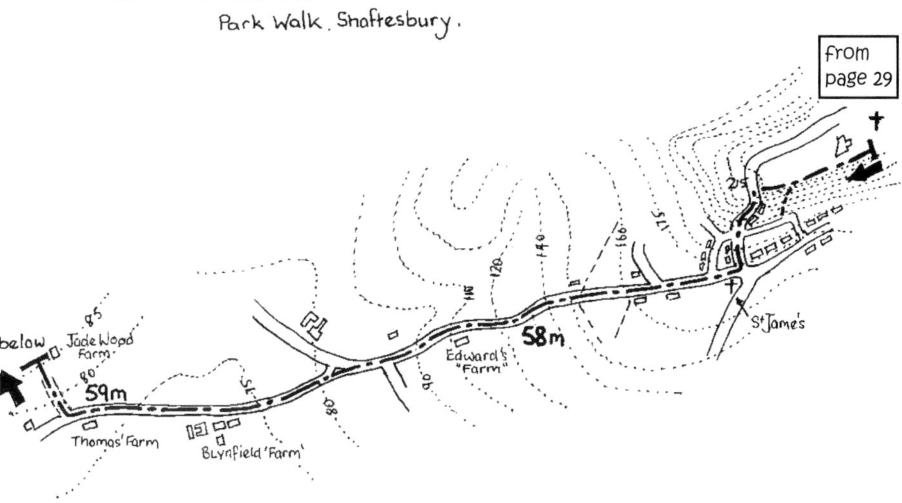

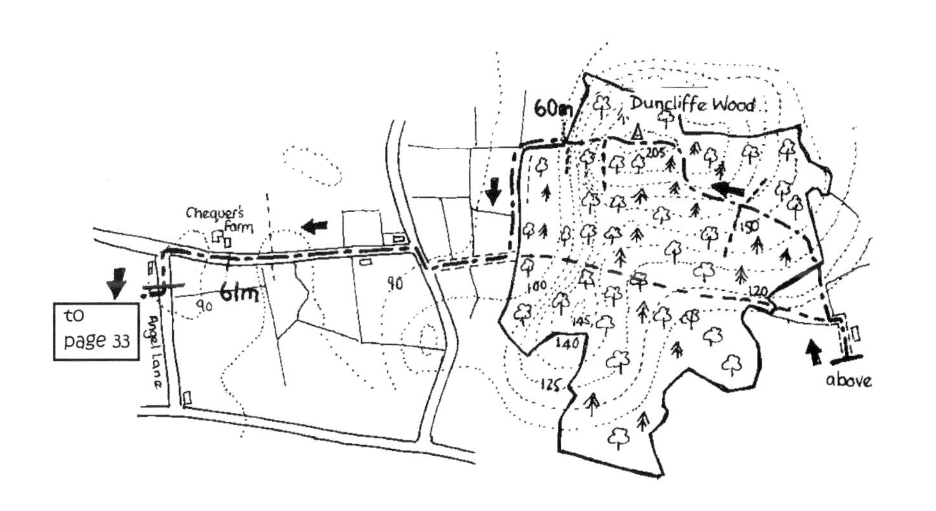

After about 50 yards along Angel Lane, at the first metal gate on the right, a path crosses the field. There is no way marker or clear path, but cross the field ¼ left towards the far corner and a gate that bears an ancient way-marker to reassure us. Continue across the next field on the same bearing towards the corner a short way ahead.

Do not be surprised if you have to negotiate an electric fence or two along here, but continue ahead holding a ditch and field edge on your left to the next corner. Search as I might, I could not find a gate or stile giving access to the next field. However there was a gap in the hedge to the right of the field corner that could be negotiated. Hopefully this inadequacy will soon be remedied.

Into the next field, move to the left and follow the hedge and fence around the field to the far left corner. Just before the corner a stile comes in from the left. Further reassured, continue through the gap ahead. Initially keep to the left of the field through a gap in a barbed wire fence and beyond that towards the middle of the fence that terminates the next field. From here a double stile and bank descend into a small pasture, across which, through a gate, a small lane passes between homes, to the busy B3092.

Stour Provost is gained by turning left and then, shortly after, right. It is the very epitome of the English village, but a community that provides nothing in the way of provisions for the weary traveller. Having looked around then, head south along Butts Lane for twenty or thirty yards to a stile on the right.

From atop the stile, the view opens out to the southwest, and St Gregory's Church in Marnhull stands as a beacon on the skyline. A series of fields, each with a stile or two to climb, indicate the way ahead, initially to the left and then continuing in a southerly direction. Across the fourth field, aim for the gate, at an angle in the field, that leads to a stile. The larger field beyond the stile may be subject to ploughing or heavy planting, and the path across it (half right) may not be clear. It may therefore be advisable to go around the field, anticlockwise, to the stile just left of the far right corner.

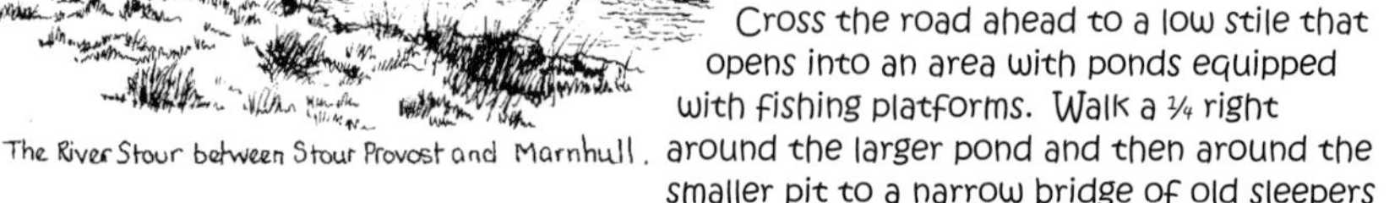
The River Stour between Stour Provost and Marnhull.

Cross the road ahead to a low stile that opens into an area with ponds equipped with fishing platforms. Walk a ¼ right around the larger pond and then around the smaller pit to a narrow bridge of old sleepers beyond it. This leads in turn to a stile and another field. Go right and around the field, now alongside a very young River Stour. It is hard to imagine that this is the same mature river that we had for company in Christchurch so many miles before. At another stile, continue in pleasant circumstances across the grass meadow alongside the river. Keep the fence close on your left. The meadow ends at a stile in the distant left corner, alongside cottages. There is an obvious footbridge across the other side of the meadow.

At the road, turn initially left and then, opposite a cemetery, cross a stile on the right beneath a chestnut tree and head down the field to a break in the hedge on the right. Through this, turn left across the field towards an old house (Haines) and the stile in front of it. Turn right at the road and after a few paces climb the steps on the left to a narrow path between the houses. When the path meets a large field, climb ¼ left up the field, beyond the trees to the fence and hedgerow ahead. Go through a stile and gate and descend ¼ left, across wet ground, towards the far left corner of the field where a kissing gate and houses herald our arrival in 'The Largest Village In England' – Marnhull. Turn to the right towards the main street through the village.

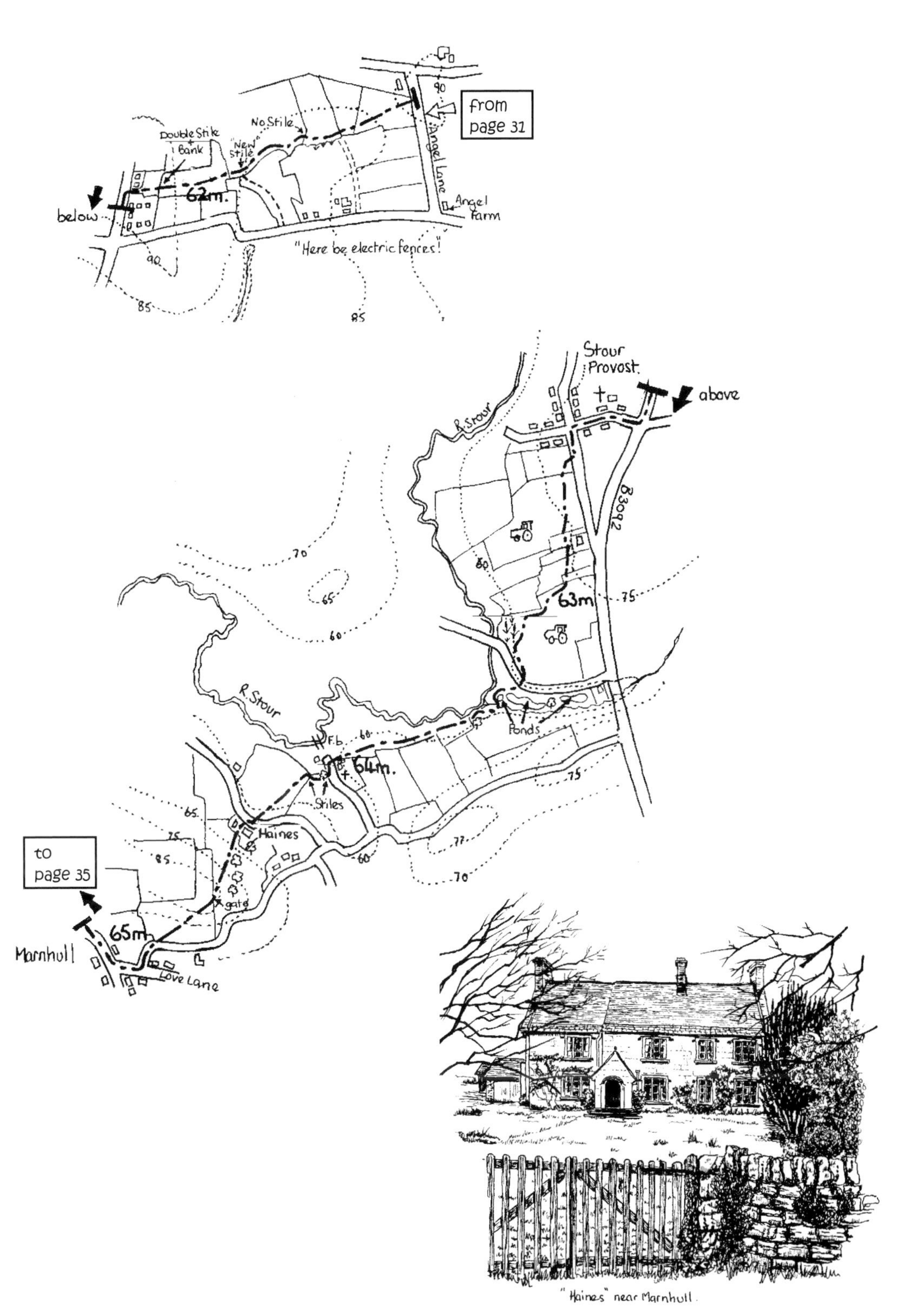

"Haines" near Marnhull.

Marnhull to Sherborne. (11 Miles)

The Crown Inn. Marnhull.

We arrive in Marnhull via Love Lane. Marnhull provides well for the walker, with the Crown Inn to the south of the village and the Blackmore Vale Inn in the north. (It is from here that we take our leave.) Both the village and pubs have a 'Hardy connection'. Marnhull was apparently Marlott in 'Tess of the D'Urbevilles' (the birth place of Tess). Hardy called the Crown 'The Pure Drop Inn' and the Blackmore Vale he called 'Rollivers'.

We take our leave of the village by turning right from Love Lane (heading northwest), on the way passing a small parade of shops, (at which victuals may be purchased), and the Blackmore Vale Inn. Beyond the Pub, the road takes a turn to the right. Here take the lesser road (Ham Lane) on the left to its end in about ¼ mile. When the tarmac comes to an end, turn left into the field (not the apparent track alongside the bungalow), and descend alongside the hedgerow to the lower corner. There is a bridle path sign coming in from the right at this point. Here, turn to the left stepping through the mud as you do so. Through the gap, the path turns immediately to the right, westerly (approx 260°), on the left hand side of the hedgerow.

Cross the stile to a little-used footbridge. The wooden slats that form the bridge are beginning to show signs of wear, do not jump up and down! Instead hurry onwards to cross the River Stour (grown a little larger since last we saw it.). From here, head across the field, with the river snaking along your right, to a double stile and ditch in the fence. Continue on to the next stile across an electric fence and beyond that to yet another old double stile and ditch. After another two fields and their stiles, cross the largest of the fields to a stile in the middle of the hedgerow at its furthest end. Over this one, head half left across the field towards the cottages and farm in the far corner. A gate opens to a junction of lanes alongside Triangle Farm. Take the lane opposite.

Rather than searching out a footpath that is supposed to leave alongside Triangle Farm towards Priors Down, head instead along the country lane towards Stalbridge (1¼m) and save yourself some time.

As Stalbridge is approached it begins to take on the appearance of an industrial estate, but do not be dismayed as it offers much for the walker. With a bank, post office, butcher, pub and fish and chip shop (closed on Sundays and Mondays), there is every excuse not to hurry on unless time is pressing.

Cross the A357 and continue up the hill, ignoring a road alongside the houses on the right. After a ¼ mile, when you reach Wood Lane on the left, turn down it and after a 100 yards, take a footpath on the right. Along Wood Lane there are fine retrospective views to be had across the Blackmore Vale.

Pass through the kissing gate and continue across the field alongside an electric fence towards the corner of the woodland. Through another kissing gate, continue straight ahead on a footpath alongside an ivy-covered and decrepit wall, to a stile at the end of the wood at which point views open up ahead considerably. Follow the hedge line on your right down to a stile in the next corner.

The path now descends steeply, half right, across a spring and towards a bend in a road but before it is reached, cross a stile to the left that leads away from the road. Cross a second stile, and take the path to the right (southwest).

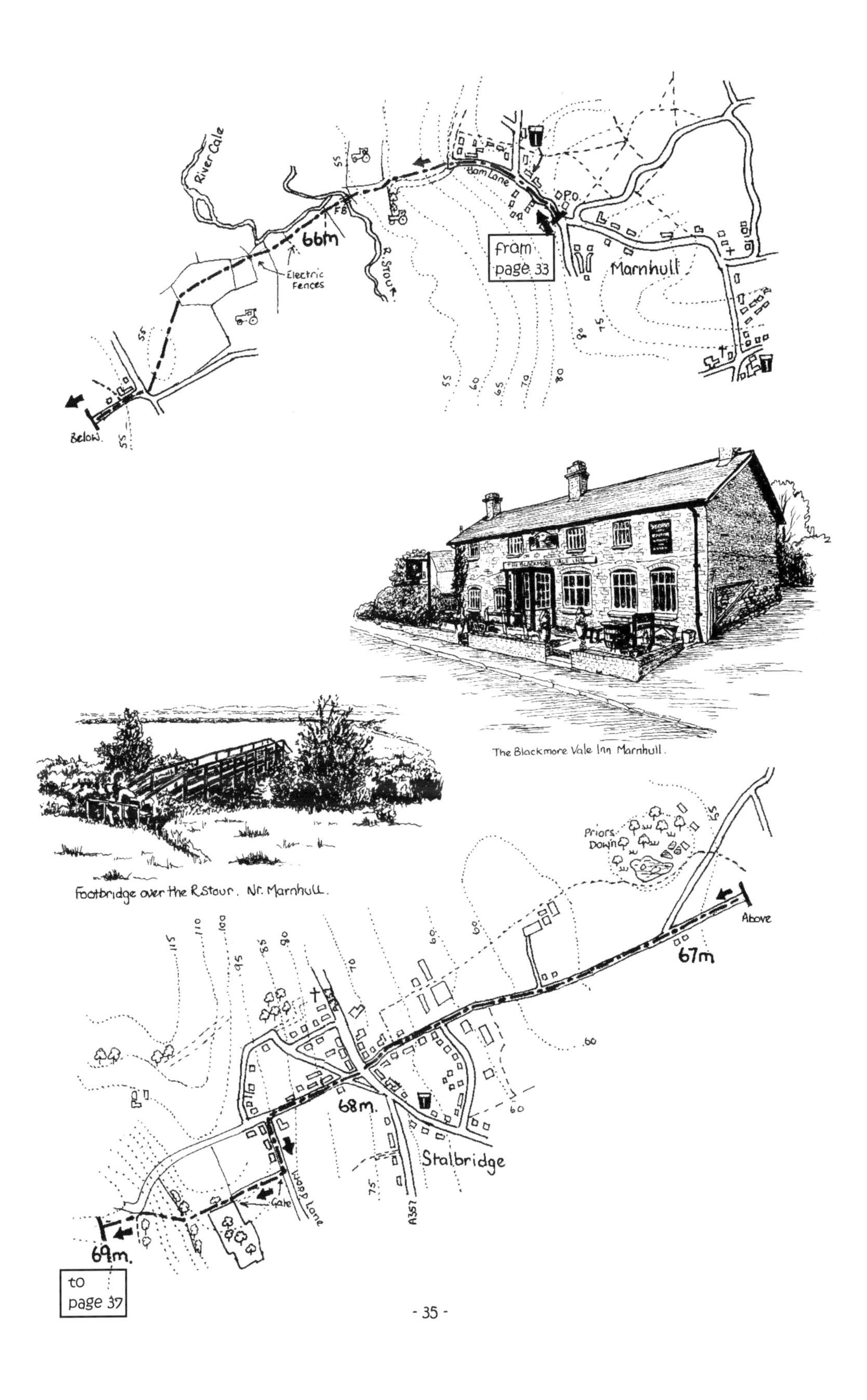

The Blackmore Vale Inn Marnhull.

Footbridge over the R.Stour. Nr. Marnhull.

A path crosses this field towards a stile that emerges on to a minor road. Head left for a while until, as you top a short rise, you arrive at a stile and gate on the right. The path continues alongside a wooded area (Church Close) with a minor valley on the right. With the sun setting in the west, this is a pleasant little walk.

Continue ahead through a succession of three gates. After a short section of isolated hedgerow, before a fence obstructs the direction of walk, turn to the left towards a metal farm gate onto a tarmac farm road and here turn to the right. For a while this offers easy walking with extensive views over thoughtfully, low cut hedgerows. But as Manor Farm is passed the road surface begins to break up whilst becoming liberally coated with a glutinous mix of mud and farmyard manure, (especially after rain) which continues until the track begins to rise onto higher ground.

The path deteriorates further after a gate, but continues in the same direction (northwest) towards trees ahead. Through the next gate continue ahead across the grassy field past an old solitary oak tree. The field path descends to the far left corner where we encounter a spring, which has created a muddy cleft. This ends at a gate into narrow and often overgrown path that descends to the gardens and houses of Clayhanger. At the road, turn left up the hill alongside Plumley Wood .

After about ¼ mile, as the crest of the hill is approached, there is a bridle path on the right. This path runs initially alongside the road then, once through an old rickety gate, passes a cottage then fields, with Plumley Wood all-the-while on your right. Though initially clear, the path soon becomes less well used. Provided you do not stray down the slope on the right no problems will be experienced (except nettles). Continue to walk to the south, through two gates along the way, (which define a small area of conservation) until a roadway is met in ½ mile.

Turning right, walk along Rue Lane for a mile due west. When you can, glimpse the views to the north.

The lane descends to a junction at which head initially to the left, but shortly after, turn right to a gate and footpath. Continue ahead, across and up the slope towards the tree line. Pass the first gate and walk alongside the tree line above the valley, to a second, older gate. Pass through this (or over it). With the trees now on your right and walking in the same direction, approach Coach Hill Wood straight ahead.

In the corner of the field pass through a wooden gate into the wood. Turn slightly left along the forest track. After a ¼ mile, when the track makes a clear turn to the right, a little used but rustic wrought iron gate straight ahead provides our exit. Continue through it and to the right, alongside the edge of the wood.
Hidden in the corner of the field a stile reveals the way ahead across a small valley.

Descend the field, ¼ right, to the fence below. (The path over the next field is revealed as a diagonal scar going to the left.) At the bottom of the field, cross the stile and a tricky plank bridge through the hedge, then continue up the next field to a stile and the road beyond.

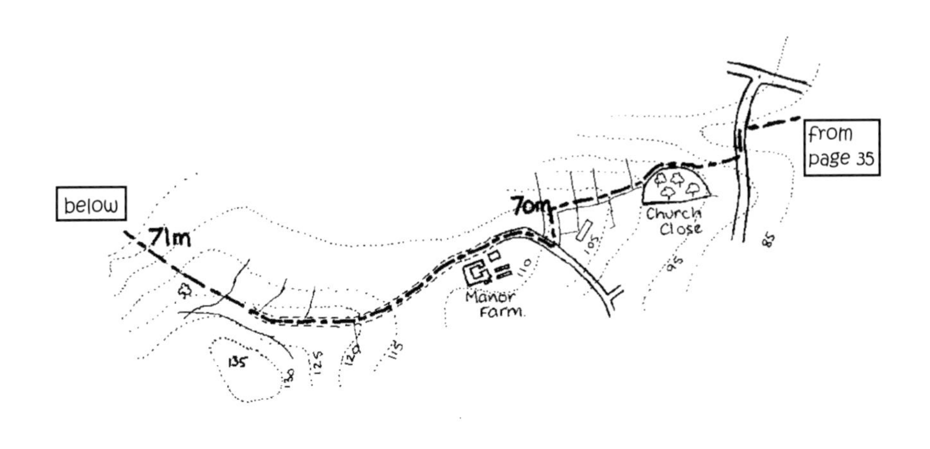
from
page 35
below
71m
70m
Church
Close
Manor
Farm
85
95
105
110
115
120
125
130
135

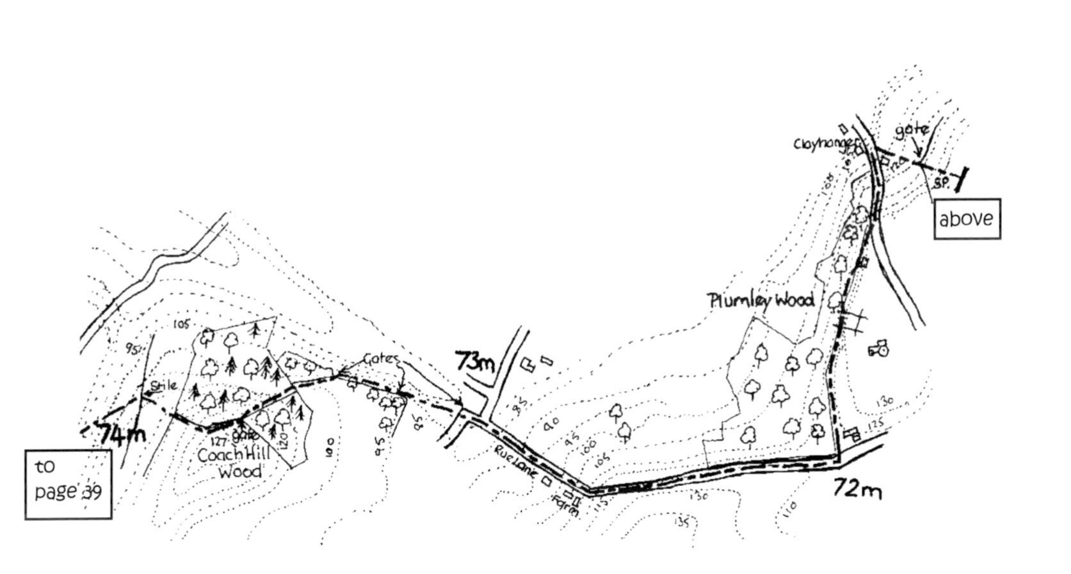
Clayhanger
gate
SP
above
Plumley Wood
72m
73m
Gates
Rue Lane
Farm
Stile
74m
gate
127
Coach Hill
Wood
to
page 39
105
95
120
100
130
125
135
110

Turn initially left alongside the estate wall, to the ornate wrought iron gates (and rather special kissing gate!) that provide a grand entrance to what is described as 'The Camp' on the OS map. Note the attractive cottage at the gateway, once the gamekeeper's cottage, and the first of two. This one is in use.

The day ends memorably in the estate associated with Sherborne Castle. This section begins along a tarmac road, in parkland, arriving shortly at a fork from which we turn ¼ left into a private woodland towards a collection of sheds and hangers that indicate the use to which the woods and the land are now put. In front of a large corrugated shed turn to the left. Behind the shed a concrete path provides echoes of the area's military past.

When the path makes a turn to the left, continue on ahead with the trees now on your right. This path cuts across the corner of the woodland and arrives at a deer fence and appropriately high gateway, which exits the wood heading west, towards an area called Jerusalem or more correctly Jerusalem Hill.

As the pathway descends, look around you. Remember, you are in an ancient deer park and its inhabitants may make an appearance amongst the trees.

The path descends to a second gamekeeper's cottage (Middle Lodge). This one is not in use but looks like something out of Hansel and Gretel. Alongside it another tall gate leads out of the parkland, still heading west, onto a clear track.

The track makes for easy walking to both the feet and the eye, and follows the contour of a hill that is topped with woodland (Old Park). It continues ahead for over ½ mile until it turns down to Sherborne Castle itself and affords unequalled views down to the Castle and lake.

Sherborne Castle

Here our route leaves the main track and takes a footpath ahead, across a field up to a tall, spiked, metal kissing gate. Go through this and walk down the grass track, in parkland, to run parallel with the main road and access road to the Sherborne Castle estate (New Road). The path descends gently down to the road itself at the point at which a junction turns into the town of Sherborne.

Sherborne is a town of interest and history and offers refreshment in plenty. You will need to be made of strong stuff to turn away from it.

Sherborne Old Castle.

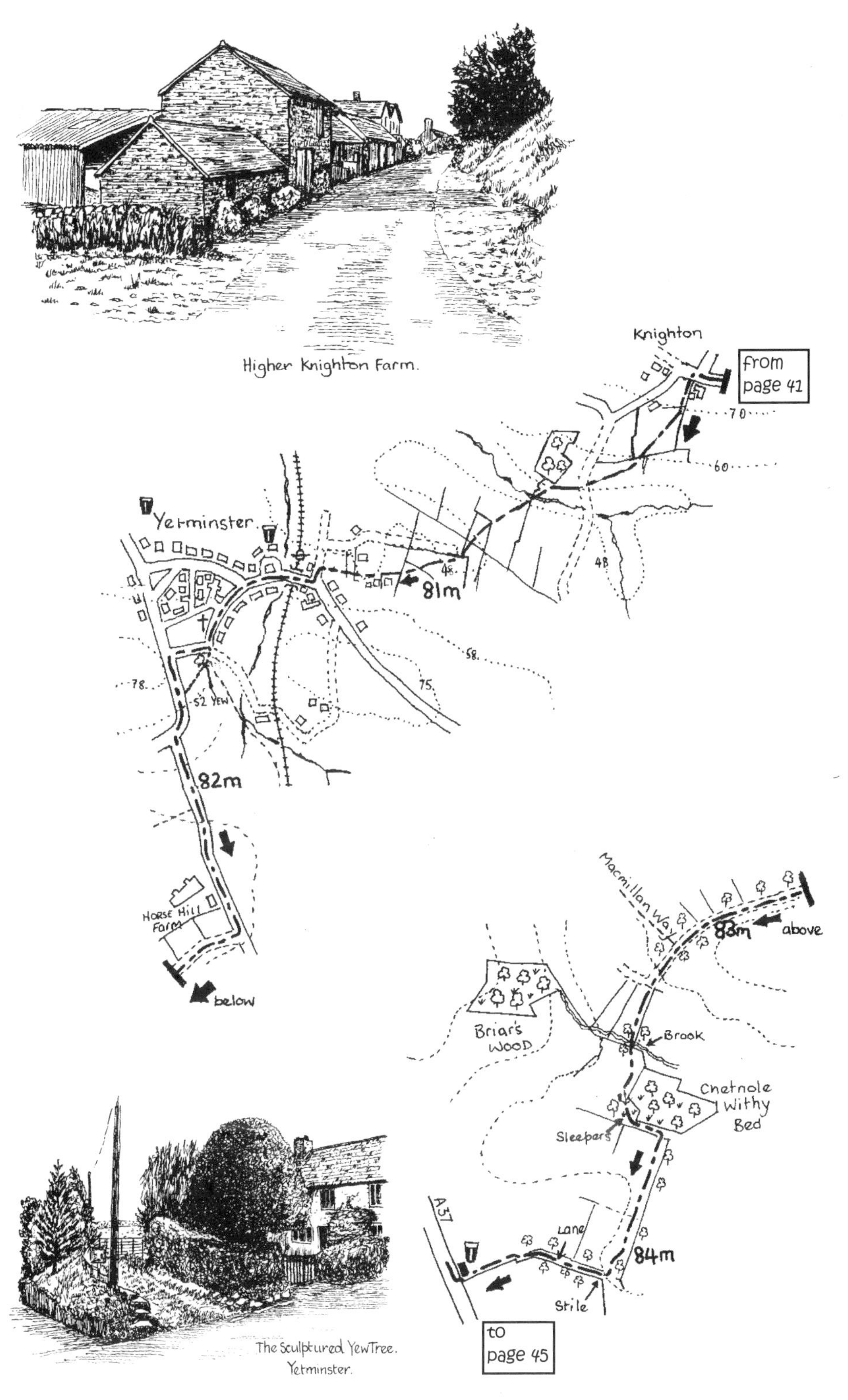
Higher Knighton Farm.
Knighton
from page 41
70
60
Yetminster
48
81m
58
78
75
52 YEW
82m
HORSE HILL Farm
below
Macmillan Way
83m
above
Briar's WOOD
Brook
Chetnole Withy Bed
Sleepers
A37
Lane
84m
Stile
to page 45
The Sculptured Yew Tree. Yetminster.

The Water splash. Melbury Osmond.

On stepping out of the pub turn to the right. Shortly after, cross the road to a stile into a field. After meeting a fence, turn right to a double stile and the road to Melbury Osmond. Turn left.

As the road begins to climb, turn left to a gate and path alongside Meads Cottage. After a second gate, the path passes between gardens and makes a right turn, shortly to arrive at the road. Turn left and walk down to a ford or water splash. (In an effort to clean off muddy boots, the author strode through the water only to slip on the algae covered cobbles and flipped 'base over apex' into the stream. Standing there dripping wet I made a note to encourage you to elect for the small footbridge instead).

Melbury Osmond is a picturesque village, with a church and cluster of thatched cottages, but instead of further exploration, I chose to march on in order to dry off, warm up and hide my embarrassment, most probably to my loss.

The road (which, in a short while turns to the left, and then sharply right at Towns End), ends at a cattle grid and there begins, unannounced, an enchanting stroll through the parkland of Melbury House. The tarmac road that serves as its drive is our footpath for more than 1½ miles. It approaches, and then passes the grand house itself and the church of Melbury Sampford.

The gates of Melbury Park.

The ease of travel provides an opportunity to enjoy the surroundings and travel a little more rapidly than we have become accustomed, so we have time for a little history. The house was built in the 16th c. and is the home of the Earls of Ilchester, the Fox Strangeways family. The current occupant is the Honourable Charlotte Townsend. The deer park, established in 1546, is still much in evidence, and once beyond the house, aside from the views of the lake, you might catch a glimpse of the deer themselves. For those of you that arrive here in the late autumn, (the rutting season) the visit may prove to be especially memorable.

The house is rounded to the right and the drive then climbs to its highest point, and descends again to the main gates near Evershot. Note the lions (circa 1690) that adorn the gate piers. Continue down the lane to a T-junction. Turn right at the junction and walk through the village.

St Osmond's Church Evershot.

Walking up West Hill, the road passes the road to the charmingly Dorset sounding Girt Farm. (For those unaccustomed to the Dorset dialect, girt means large or great.) Our route continues on the main road and soon begins to descend to Horsey Knapp During the descent, the distinctive hill off to the north and conspicuous in the middle distance, with the motte and bailey earthworks, is Castle Hill at East Chelborough.

At the next junction, turn right on to the road to 'Chelborough'. After a further ½ mile, go straight over a junction towards 'West Chelborough'.

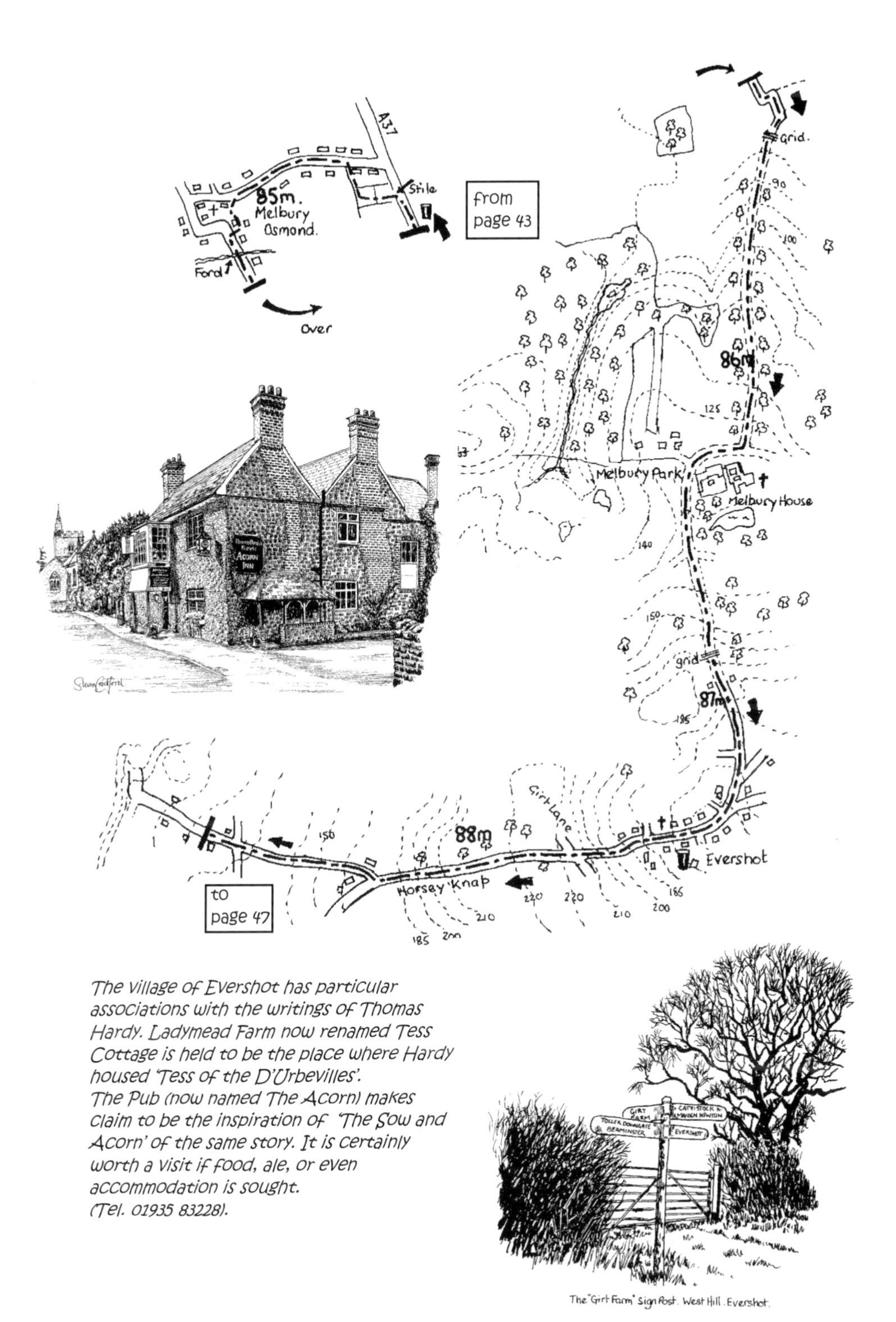

The village of Evershot has particular associations with the writings of Thomas Hardy. Ladymead Farm now renamed Tess Cottage is held to be the place where Hardy housed 'Tess of the D'Urbevilles'. The Pub (now named The Acorn) makes claim to be the inspiration of 'The Sow and Acorn' of the same story. It is certainly worth a visit if food, ale, or even accommodation is sought. (Tel. 01935 83228).

The "Girt Farm" Sign Post. West Hill. Evershot.

As the road rises to a minor summit and to a sharp bend to the right, turn left on to the track towards Hemlock Farm. Almost immediately a bridle path sign indicates our way up a muddy bank on the right, a path made muddy by the hooves of many horses. This path rises steeply to a gate into a meadow and so, half right, up to the high ground. Alongside the fence pass through another gate and continue ahead, on still steadily rising ground with ever improving views.

Now on Chelborough Hill, we should find ourselves approaching what appears to be a set of standing stones. Do not be deceived, there is something very contemporary about these and I cannot guarantee their continued existence. If they are not there when you pass by, don't blame me. Beyond this a double gate serves as a better guide.
Beyond the gate, do not turn down to the left, but instead continue straight ahead along the fence line to the right of farm buildings in the far corner of the field. Once alongside the buildings continue on a 'drove', soon to become a muddy lane. Along here the ground falls away steeply on the right.
Through a gate with a hurdle to its right, carry on through a second gate and so into the muddy lane. After a few hundred yards or so, the lane takes a turn to the left to follow the Hardy's Way. At this point go straight ahead, through a gate and across a meadow, aiming ¼ right to descend to a stile decorated with barbed wire thoughtfully wrapped in plastic bin liners to protect those with shorter legs. The path descends a steep bank to the right. A route diversion soon directs us across a stile on the left towards a cottage. Pass around the cottage (Norwood Cottage) to the left and follow the footpath, running parallel to the road, through a series of meadows to arrive, providentially, alongside the Fox Inn. The Fox Inn is a lovely little pub and if your timing is good will provide a welcome break, (accommodation available Tel / Fax. 01935 891330)

The Fox Inn, Corscombe.

Turn to the right in front of the Fox and in a hundred yards or so turn left into a gated driveway alongside Corscombe Court, a 13th-14th century manor house that, according to the OS map, once boasted a moat. The path continues straight ahead to a metal gate. There are no footpath signs, but in a muddy pasture, cross the field a ¼ right to a metal gate. Now go ahead towards a gap in a new plantation. At the top of the field, you will descend to a gate and into a narrow lane. Turn to the left to climb, for a ¼ mile, back towards Corscombe.

At the road, on a bend alongside the Pines, turn right. Descend through the village and at the junction, turn with the road to the right. Just a little further on turn left into a lane opposite Knapp Farm. Almost immediately, turn right alongside a cottage, into a field. Cross the field to a gate ahead. The footpaths here-abouts are little used and unclear but the footpath continues across the next two fields towards a gate in the hedgerow. Beyond this there is a vague path, descending the field (¼ left). Do not follow this, but go straight towards the tree line at the bottom of the field. There, search for a wooden footbridge across the brook that runs along the shallow wooded valley. Over this, ascend the field towards Weston Manor Farm.
Aim to the left of the farm buildings. There go left to a stile (little used) and a gap in the wall. Through that, continue left round the buildings, through a network of metal pens, to a meeting of ways alongside the farmhouse itself. A clear track heading left through a gate (south west) provides delight to the eyes and easy walking.

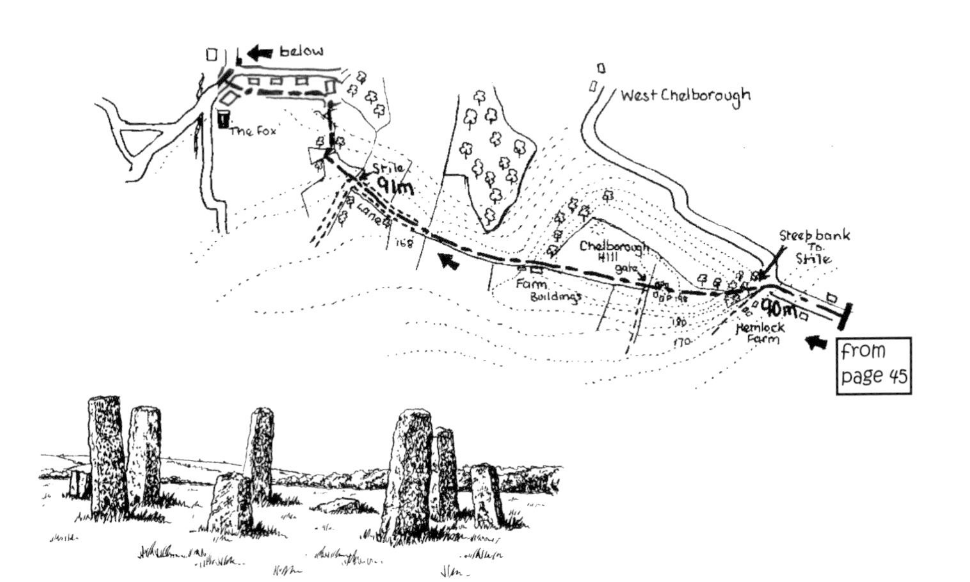

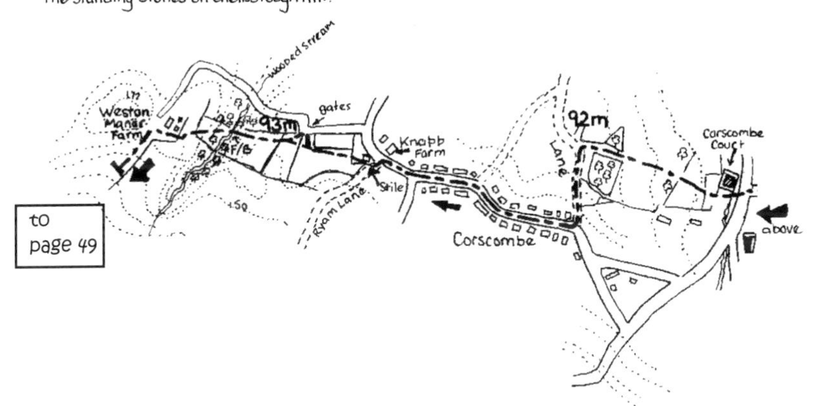

The Standing Stones on Chelborough Hill.

Weston Manor Farm.

After a ¼ mile along a broad ridge, at a collection of gates, turn to the right to continue along a grass path below the high ground on your left, as it rises slowly to the charming Hunters Lodge Farm a little under a mile ahead. After the difficulties of the day, this section is a real tonic. The track rises to the farm, which we pass to the left through a series of gates. Beyond the house, in an idyllic setting, the track becomes more formal and rises to the busyA356. Turn right towards Winyard's Gap.

The road soon turns to the left to pass through the ridge of high ground. The cutting through which the road passes gives the location, and the pub on the other side, its name. Turn to the left around the pub and walk along the road towards Chedington, shortly to pass a house on the right with an impressive garden pond. Beyond this, go right at a conspicuous fingerboard indicating the River Parrett Trail. (The spelling of this seems at odds with the nearby 'South Perrott'. All answers welcome). The Trail is immediately rewarding, entering as it does an area that is elegant and park-like, and an equestrian playground.

The path initially follows the higher ground of the field before slowly descending on grass with extensive views to the west. Maintain the same direction through a series of gates. Do not be deviated even when, beyond one of these gates, a muddy path turns off to the right. Instead continue across the field, half right, passing a row of oaks and descend to a gate in the far right corner.

At the bottom of the next field a well-made farm track heads off to the right. (Manor Farm). Do not follow this, but continue slightly left along the bottom of the next field to its far corner. Once through the gate, turn to the right to a stile into the next field. Cross the field ½ left to a most unique stile. It is truly a 'stile with style', and leads, somewhat unexpectedly, round a play area with climbing frames and things. Go initially left, and then turn right around the play area. Follow the fence to a track and bridge over a stream. A lane now heads towards South Perrott. When I passed this way, much of the lane had been turned into a river, or perhaps a river had adopted the lane as an easier route. Whatever, the route is obvious (if wet), and ends at the southern end of the village.

Langmore Lane. South Perrott.

At the road ahead turn to the right. South Perrott can be short circuited by a path on the left to the church, otherwise continue to the A356 and turn left. In a couple of hundred yards the Coach & Horses is passed on the left. The Baker's Arms on the right is now a private dwelling, though the sign remains. Opposite the Baker's Arms, a delightful, fern-clad path leads off to the left, between cottages and alongside a brook. Keep to the left of the brook to a stone slab bridge. Across the 'bridge', pass through a metal gate on to Langmore Lane, a track heading southwest towards Mosterton.

In reasonably dry conditions, the going is easy. After a ¼ mile or so however, the path makes a clear turn to the right and begins to descend to a stream in an increasingly muddy environment. Shortly beyond this the path narrows again and necessitates turning into the field on the right to walk alongside the field to a stile in the corner. Continue across the next pasture to a gap in the hedgerow opposite and continue, ¼right, to a stile up in the high point of the next pasture. On slightly more open ground, go round the field edge to yet another stile and from there cross the field ahead to a gate and minor road into the village. Turn to the right to meet the A3066. To leave Mosterton turn to the right.

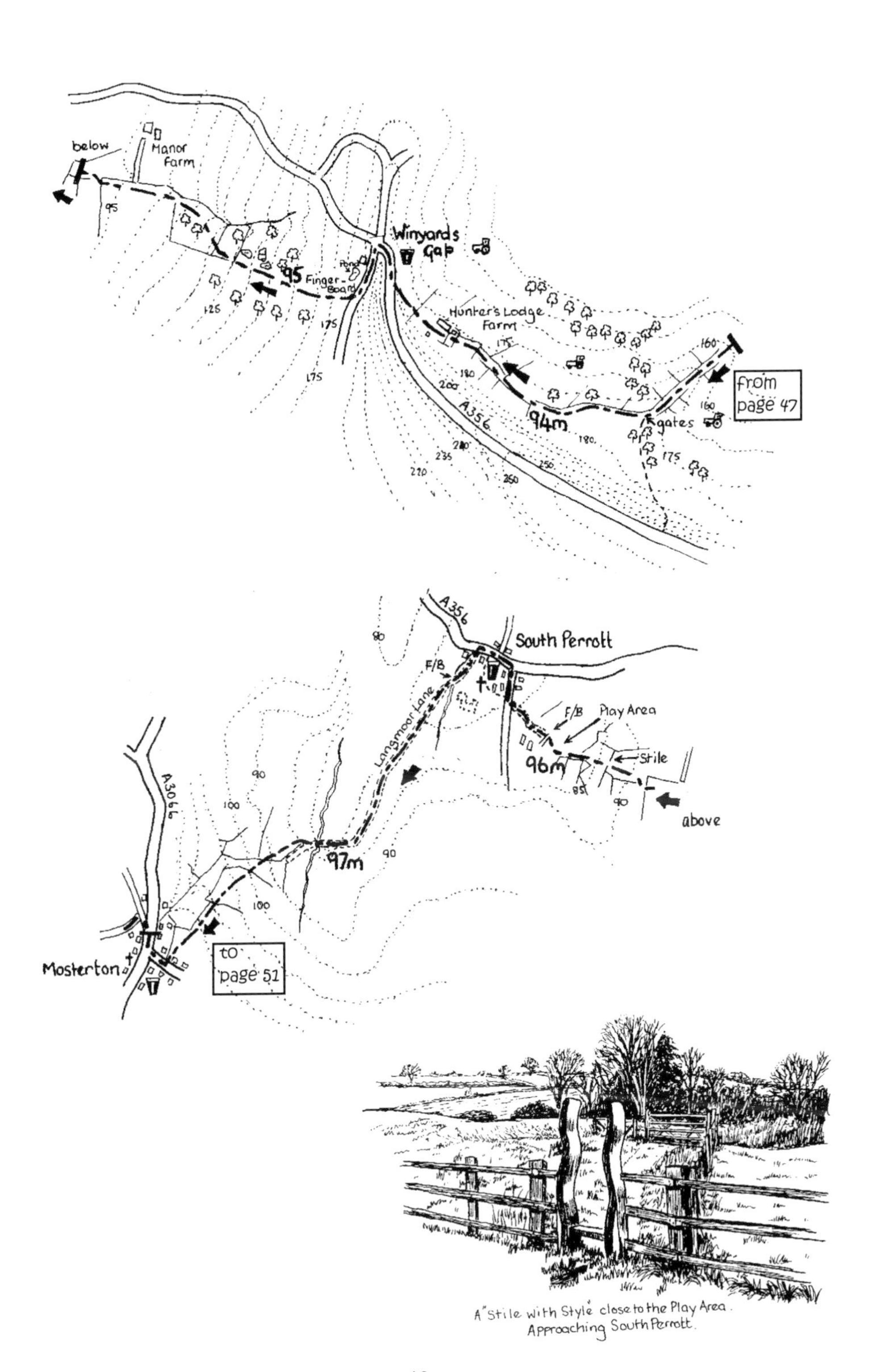

A "Stile with Style" close to the Play Area. Approaching South Perrott.

After 100 yards, turn left on to Down Road, and shortly after left again on the metalled track towards West Farm. This farm road rises gently for a little under a mile with increasingly open ground to the south.

Pass through the farmyard (possibly in the company of farmyard dogs) to the left of the house to a fence line and gate. Avoid the first gate and instead take the one to its right, and walk in the same direction as before, along the field edge to a gate and fingerboard in the left hand corner of the field. The fingerboard points our way to Seaborough, so head off across the field slightly right towards the telegraph poles that adorn it and roughly point the way to a clear farm track. (The conspicuous hill off to the southwest is Pilsdon Pen, the high point of this stretch of the journey.)

The track passes through the farm, made 'atmospheric' by the presence of livestock and a prize slurry pit. Descend to the minor road ahead. Don't be deviated on to the track immediately left, but go on to the road itself at a bend. Turn initially left, and follow the road as it turns to the right, soon passing the church (St Johns), into the village of Seaborough. At the junction, turn to the left and walk down the hill for 300 yards.

Pass the first bridle path on the right, and continue down the road over a stream and look for a footpath (Monarchs Way) through the hedge on your right. Over the stile, head slightly left towards the far corner of the field (around 243°). There is a farm conversion on your left. The impressive home occupying the high ground to the right (north) is Seaborough Court.

Head to a stile, over which continue on towards the tree ahead and a gate in a corner of the next field. Continue along the fence line, half left, to the next gate and then, in the same direction, follow the fence line round to a gate on your right on to a small green lane or 'drove'. Turn left along the drove and soon after, turn through a metal gate. Now head ¼ right towards a gap in the hedge ahead, with the houses of Drimpton beyond.

The ground rises towards the houses and a gate in the far right hand corner. Through the gate, turn to the left to the minor road. Turn to the right past the church (St Mary's) and the pub (the Royal Oak) beyond which the road bends to the left. Follow it (avoiding the lesser 'Crewkerne Road' ahead), for a ¼ mile. Beyond the crossroads take a footpath on the left, opposite some houses (Oakland's Farm).

Cross the stile and walk around the field to the right to another stile. Now go left around the field and descend to an opening and beyond that go straight ahead, on rising ground to two stiles in the far corner. Once over the stiles, walk along the top of the field to a gate and a minor roadway, there turn to the right and follow the road beyond the farm. Pass the first road on the right and as the road makes a bend to the right, turn slightly left on to the clear but ancient track heading southwest

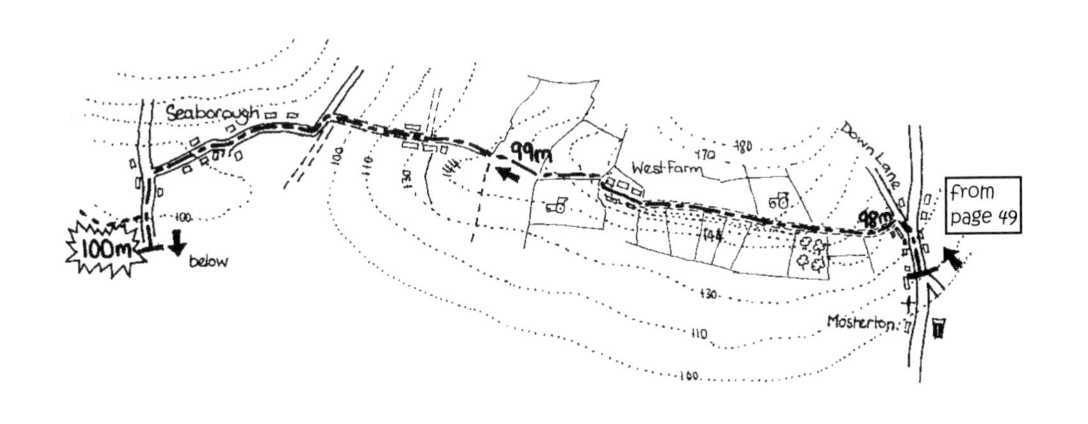
Seaborough
99m
West Farm
Down Lane
98m
from page 49
Mosterton
100m
below

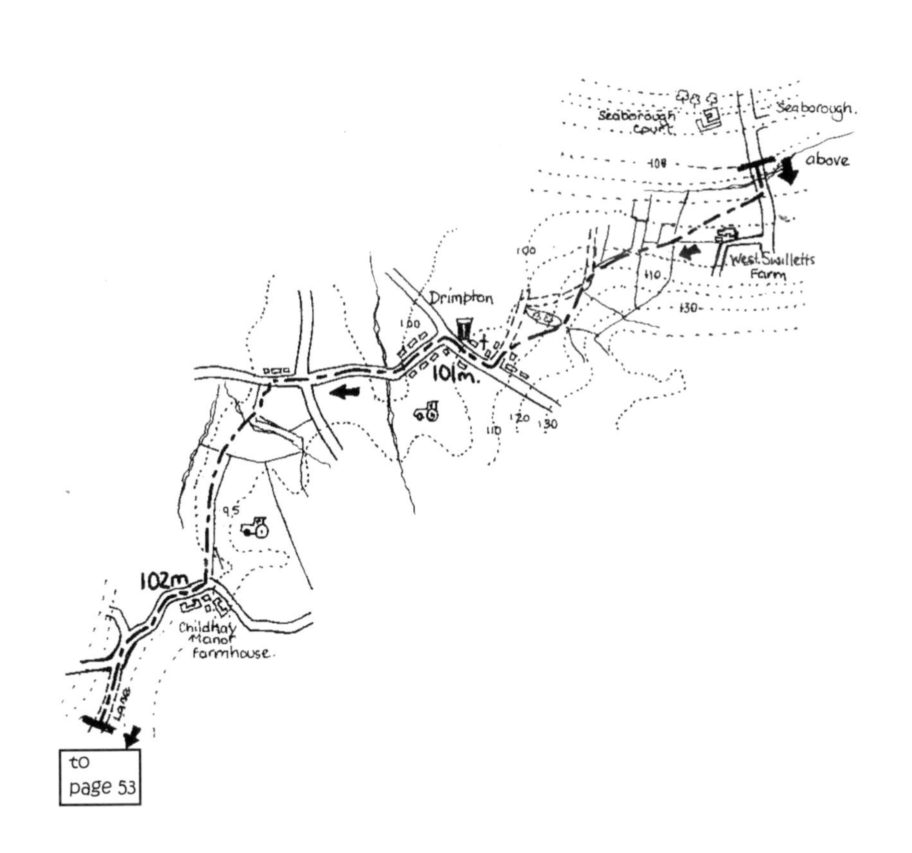
Seaborough Court
Seaborough
above
West Swilletts Farm
Drimpton
101m
102m
Childhay Manor Farmhouse
Lane
to page 53

When the track comes to an end in a tangle of undergrowth, a stile on the right enables us to maintain our direction of travel across a series of fields and stiles. Shortly a pylon looms ahead which makes for a good target. On approaching the pylon a field boundary ahead offers a choice of three gates; take the middle one, to the left of a pond set in a dip. Cross the next field to a gate that opens on to a minor road on which we turn right and walk up the hill towards Blackdown, with 'Blackdown House' on the right.

At the road junction turn to the right below the ridge of Blackdown Hill.

At a telephone box on the left, a footpath sign indicates the path on to the hill. Follow it to a stile and once over, stay to the left to find a further little-used stile in the corner of a small bramble-choked field (see note on p.53). Cut diagonally right up the hill towards the conspicuous group of pine trees on the top of the ridge. (Check the steeple on the church roof – An odd metal framework containing a bell.)

The Stile in Blackdown.

On reaching the summit of the ridge turn to the left. The path follows the grassy ridge with the fence on the right, and the hamlet of Blackdown on the left. After passing through one gate, the path approaches a corner of the fence and then turns to the right to pass through another gate. Now on the west of the fence, we descend to the left, on grass, to a roadway at Cole's Cross. (Note the weather vane on the cottage on the right.)

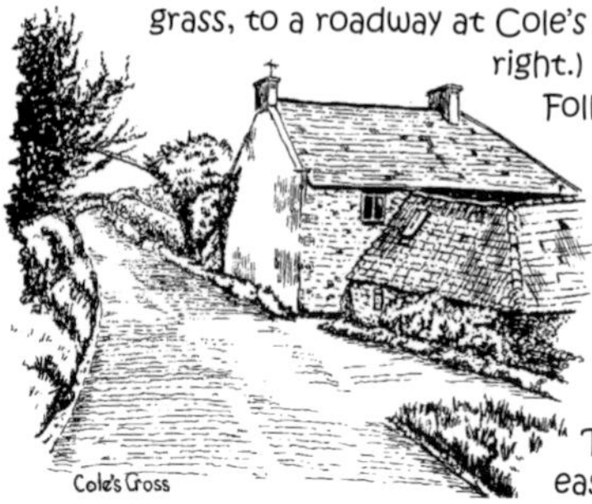

Follow the B3165 south for a ¼ mile to a grass track and gate on the left (past the village hall). This track continues ahead following the fence line until it passes through a gate at the start of the ascent to Pilsdon Pen. Immediately after the gateway turn sharply to the left and follow the route of a deeply rutted cart track alongside the fence.

The path turns right, with the fence, to head south east and continues to ascend alongside a line of elegant trees with expanding views to the left. At the gate, go through and continue ahead to the left of the next gate and climb the stile alongside the way marker. This points our way, still southeast, with the fence now on our right to the end of the field and a double stile. The indistinct path across this field does not make a bee-line for the lumps and bumps of the summit earthworks, but is on a diagonal to the right (southeast) of them, to a five bar gate.

Cole's Cross

As you cross this field take a look to your right. Is that the sea? Indeed it is.

Access to the Iron Age hill fort and summit of Pilsdon Pen lies to the right of the gate via two stiles just right of the southeast corner of the field. Descend to a gate and then climb to the left, through the banks and ditches that surround the ancient grassy plateau, to the summit of the hill.

This area is well worth taking your time to explore. The views are extensive in all directions and include views to the south and the coast with Golden Cap prominent. Dorset lies at our feet. This is, in more than one respect, a high point in our walk. Even on a bank holiday Pilsdon Pen remains a quiet retreat, little used by holidaymakers who are drawn instead to the undoubted charms of the coast.

Our descent to the road is from the southern end, alongside a trig point, to the road at a place called 'Lob Gate', for reasons best known to antiquity.

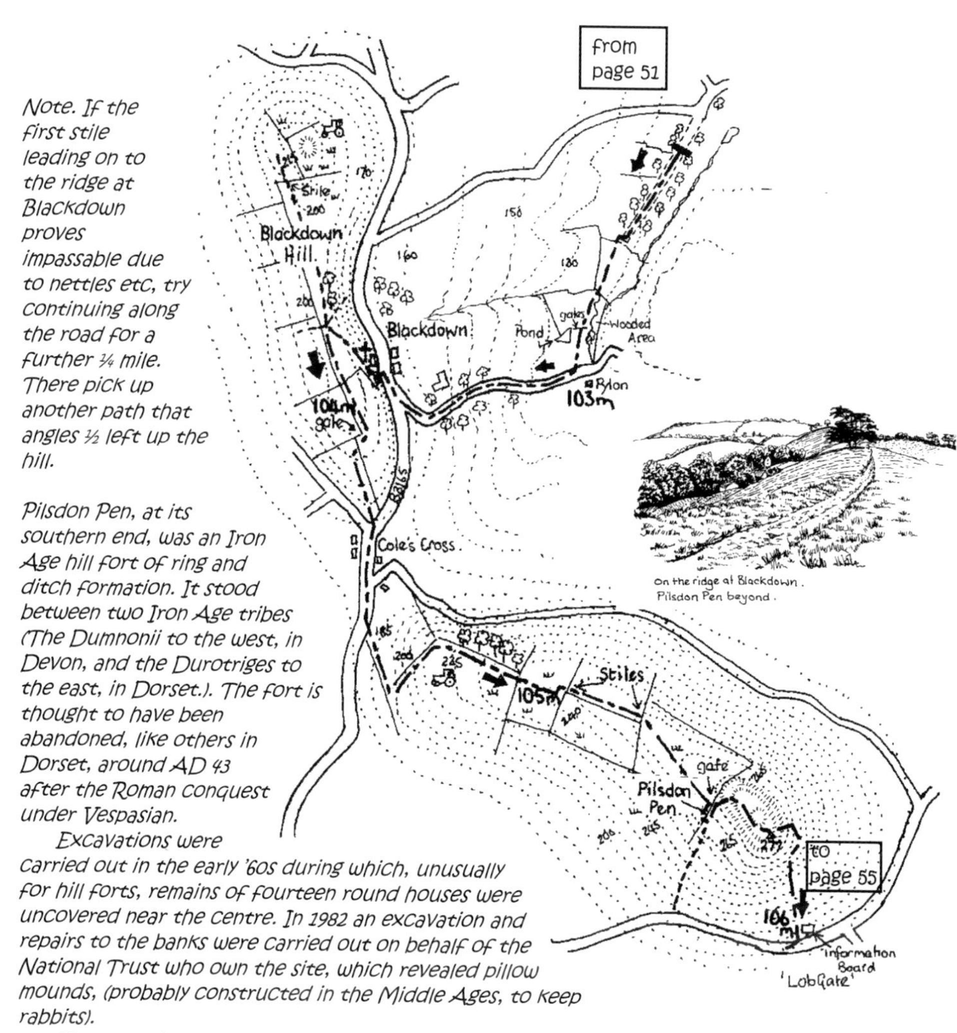

On the ridge at Blackdown. Pilsdon Pen beyond.

Note. If the first stile leading on to the ridge at Blackdown proves impassable due to nettles etc, try continuing along the road for a further ¼ mile. There pick up another path that angles ½ left up the hill.

Pilsdon Pen, at its southern end, was an Iron Age hill fort of ring and ditch formation. It stood between two Iron Age tribes (The Dumnonii to the west, in Devon, and the Durotriges to the east, in Dorset.). The fort is thought to have been abandoned, like others in Dorset, around AD 43 after the Roman conquest under Vespasian.

Excavations were carried out in the early '60s during which, unusually for hill forts, remains of fourteen round houses were uncovered near the centre. In 1982 an excavation and repairs to the banks were carried out on behalf of the National Trust who own the site, which revealed pillow mounds, (probably constructed in the Middle Ages, to keep rabbits).

There may be some doubt as to which hill is the highest point in Dorset, i.e. Pilsdon Pen or its tree-covered neighbour to the east (Lewesdon Hill), but at 908 feet, there can be no doubt that the 'pen' commands the county around it. No wonder that it was here that our ancestors chose to build their defences.

Looking South From Pilsdon Pen.

Pilsdon Pen – Charmouth (9 miles)

On arrival at the parking area on the B3164 at Lob Gate, turn to the right and follow the road as it descends for ¾ mile past Templeman's Ash. Continue past a tempting bridleway on the left (Ridgeway and Jubilee Trail), and at Attisham Farm turn left through a field gate following a right of way.

Though not immediately obvious, the path lies ahead and to the right of the fence and hedge line, heading in a southerly direction. (Do not pass through the gate immediately left, into the next field). Pass by the old metal pens and continue down the field, along the hedge line, to a gate in the bottom corner. To the right is a steep slope (Sliding Hill). Ahead and to the left is an increasingly wooded area.

Pass through the gate in the lower corner into an overgrown, but seemingly ancient sunken lane. After a short descent pass through another gate and continue alongside a field with a hedgerow on the left. The buildings of Bettiscombe Manor are soon reached. The path has been understandably diverted around the gardens alongside a high brick wall. Walk around the wall to a gate and the gravel road that serves the house. Ignoring the track to the west across a field, follow the main track up the slope to the southwest. Further walled and attractive estates soon herald our arrival at the hamlet of Bettiscombe, confirmed by a church and village hall.

Directly across the minor road, continue down a farm track to Water House Farm. The track turns slowly to the left as it descends. It then makes a turn to the right and the farm buildings come into view, (the barking of dogs may provide an early warning). Turn right, off the main track into a field, and then immediately left alongside the field's edge to a little used stile in the corner, go down to a plank bridge crossing a stream. The way emerges into an open field rising towards four trees in its centre. These turn out to be oak trees (there is also a larger, solitary specimen to the right). Walk up towards the four trees, passing to their left, and onwards towards an old gate across a muddy spring that leads into an overgrown lane that climbs and ultimately spills out on to the busy B3165.

Turn to the left along the B3165 and in a little under a mile beyond Marshwood, if it is not Monday or Tuesday lunchtime, you might anticipate a pleasant rest and some refreshment at the Bottle Inn. Along this road there is also the reward of views down through the Marshwood Vale to the sea beyond.

Continue up the road past Turner's Lane towards the wooded hill of Lambert's Castle. As the road turns to the right at the foot of the steeply wooded hill, a road to the left leads to a track that offers one route to its summit. An alternative route, slightly more direct, is a little further ahead. Continue along the road for a hundred yards. As the road begins to bend to the left, a fingerboard on the left of the road beneath an old beech tree points up a steep bank on a well-hidden path. Climb steeply, weaving around the trees, up to meet a clearer track coming from the left. Turn right, confident that it will emerge shortly, via a gate, on to the summit of the hill fort of Lambert's Castle.

Pilsdon Pen and Lewesdon Hill from Lambert's Castle.

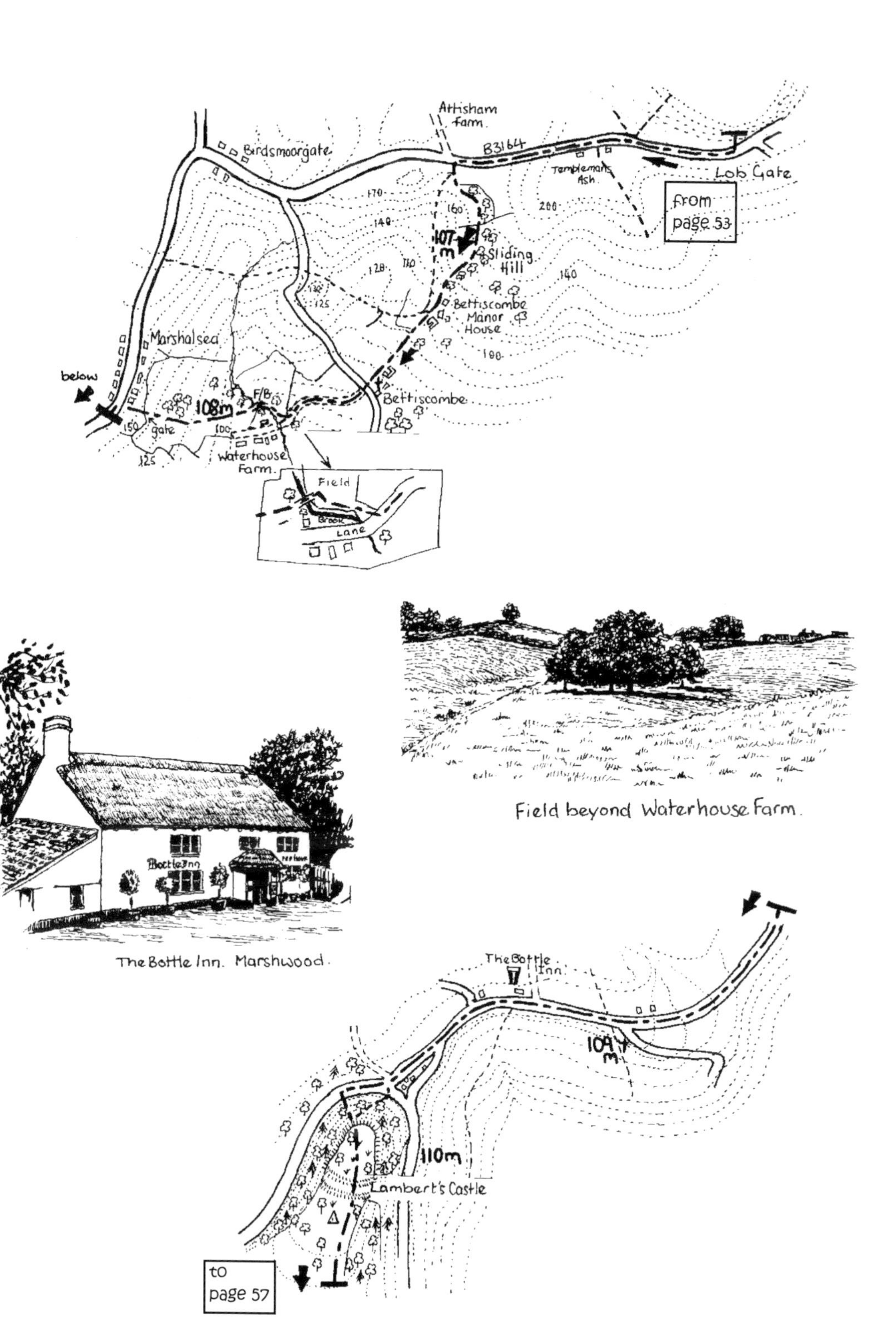

Field beyond Waterhouse Farm.

The Bottle Inn. Marshwood.

The route ahead, almost due south (around 200°), crosses a grassy plateau with views to the east and south to the coast. On a sunny day this is a wonderful spot for a picnic. It is, like most of this area, sufficiently far from the main holiday destinations away down south as to remain peaceful and undisturbed by the clamour of humanity.

At the southern end of the plateau of Lambert's Castle, the ground begins to descend on a clear sunken lane (presumably the ancient access way to the hill fort), via a five bar gate, to a confusion of minor roads. This whole area is on an elevated ridge and views remain extensive and gloriously 'Dorset' in character.

The high ground ahead (to the south) is Coney's Castle and the most obvious route is via the tarmac road over the summit. It is a route that does offer excellent views, however my chosen route lies along the track around and to the right of the summit. It starts off as a clear farm track with continuous views to the west across Fishpond Bottom towards the wooded hills of Dodpen and Wootton. Walking along here is easy and progress will be rapid.

Continue past the concrete roadway to Little Coombe Farm. In the lower reaches of this track, the Farm of Great Coombe is approached. Going gets a little sticky along here thanks to the attentions of well fed cattle, but this is soon left behind as the track climbs and emerges as a concrete road way. After a ¼mile, the minor road from the summit of Coney's Castle is met at a gate. Turn right along the road.

Within a few paces on the right, is a path that leaves the road to begin the descent to Wootton Fitzpaine. Go through the gate and descend half left along the top of the slope that sweeps down to the valley below. The path, if such there is, continues left just below a line of holly bushes, to a stile in a hedge, and from there directly across a large field (around 200°). Through a metal gate, continue half right to the corner of the next field. Ignore the gate on the right which is way marked for the Ridgeway and Liberty Trail, and instead continue, to descend to the corner of the field and another gate which opens on to a muddy lane leading down to the hamlet of Wootton Fitzpaine. The lane emerges opposite the gates of the church (adorned with unfriendly looking dogs).

Turn left along the road and in a short while turn right into the yard of Manor Farm. Walk to the far left corner where a concrete road descends to the right to the valley bottom, passing as it does, a slurry lagoon! The path soon reaches an old stone footbridge. Across this the track begins to ascend once more. Shortly after the bridge, a gate on the left gives access to the hillside and pasture of Conegar Hill.* Through this gate, head up the slope towards the clear summit of the hill to a fence line and gate just below the summit ridge. Once through the gate, a track becomes clear. Turn right along it. Again all effort is amply rewarded. This whole section commands views that will linger in the memory. The path passes by some old, wind-bent, holly trees (one now dead). It follows the fence line and contour of Conegar Hill towards the far southern corner where it meets another clearer track. Turn right to head southwest (Around 220°) along an attractive rising ridge.

The track on Conegar Hill looking South

*Note. On my last visit a fence obstructed the track in the latter stages of the walk around the summit of Conegar Hill. For an alternative, see the note on the next page.

Both Lamberts and Coney's Castle are early examples of Iron Age hill forts and are thus basic in their design when compared with others like Maiden Castle near Dorchester.

Coney's Castle was the site of a battle in the early 9th century (833 AD) between the Saxon King Egbert, King of Wessex, and a band of Danes who landed at Charmouth in 35 longships.
It seems that Egbert failed to send the Vikings back from whence they came, and having tired of pillaging and associated activities, they finally settled down to live peacefully in Charmouth.

*Note.
From the bridge at the bottom of Conegar Hill a clear farm track heads up the hill to the right of the field across which the OS map indicates a right-of-way. If you choose to do so, you may continue up this clear track and rejoin the original route at the fingerboard and the path that heads southwest on a bearing of around 220°.

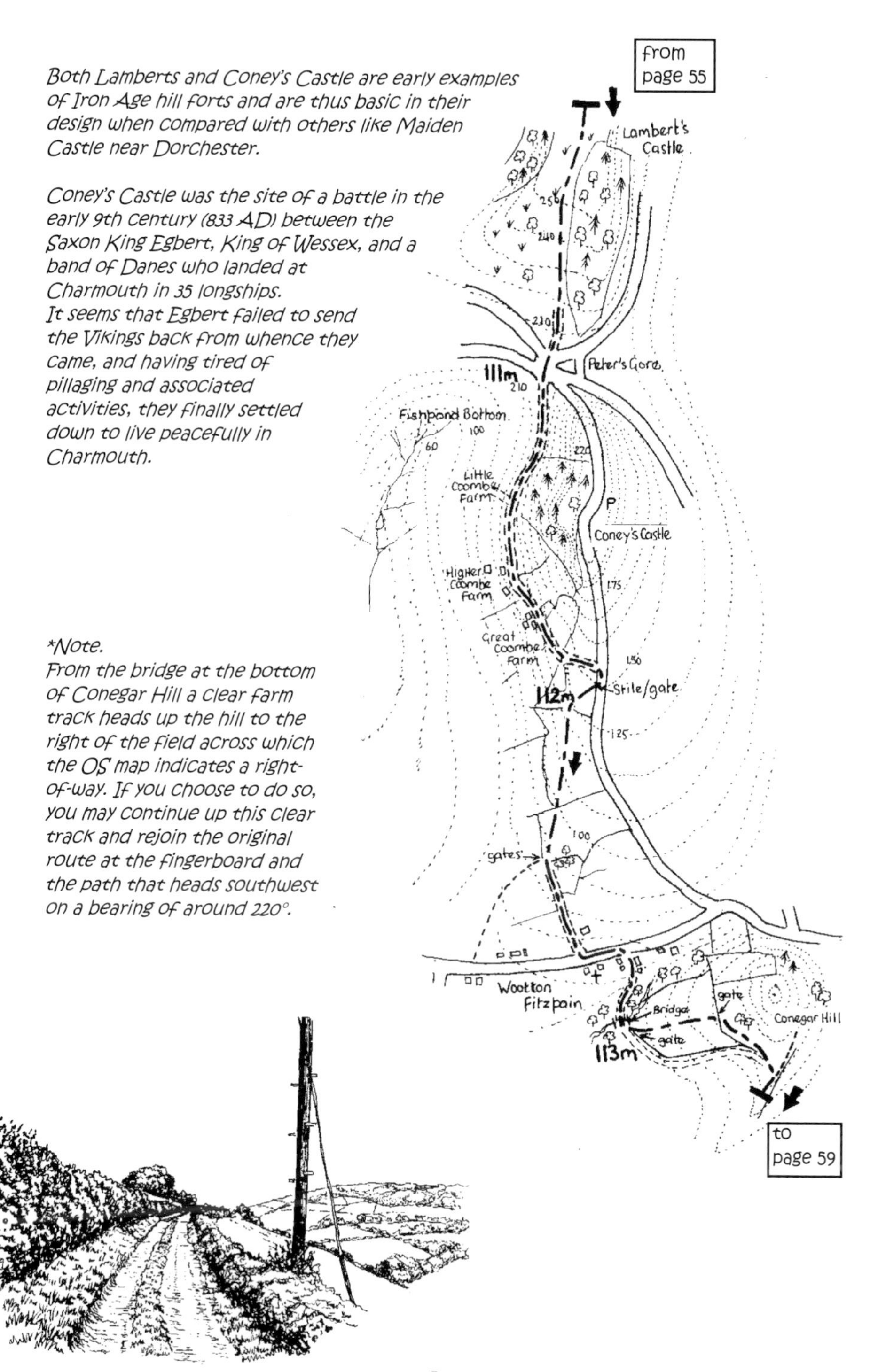

The track below Coney's Castle and towards Little Coombe Farm

The going is easy, on grass. Ignore a footpath on the left and continue alongside the fence and a distinctive row of pine trees (they have been conspicuous since reaching Conegar Hill). Charmouth is now below us and on our left.

As the path continues it descends and narrows past a copse, and arrives at a metal gate. Through the gate, continue in the same direction. The beech trees on the left, with wonderfully exposed roots are worthy of note and closer inspection. The view down towards Wootton Fitzpaine makes this a more than pleasant walk. Continue on to the woodland ahead and its access gate. The woodland has an ancient feel about it and an area of muddy ground (that has to be crossed) suggests the presence of a spring hereabouts. The path begins to narrow as it descends to the roadway.

Turn to the left and continue down the road past Little Catherston Farm (which advertises accommodation in a camping barn). As we descend this road the noisy A35 makes its presence felt. The church in Charmouth is prominent ahead.

Opposite the rather elegant portals of Catherston Manor, a little wooden gate on the right offers a route to Charmouth (½mile). Beneath a canopy of oaks, along the field edge, a path descends towards a modern road bridge in the far corner, over which passes the A35. Before you reach the bridge, pass through a kissing gate in the bottom right hand corner of the field and cross a smaller bridge with stream beneath. The path, now narrow, continues below the A35 until it meets with the Monarch's Way running north-south.

The 'Portals' of Catherston Manor.

Here a choice must be made. At the time of writing, all footpaths from Lyme Regis to Charmouth had been closed due to landslides. Unless advanced planning has been done, and the routes assured, sadly it may be expedient to by-pass the not inconsiderable charms of Lyme Regis and instead turn down into Charmouth for a well-earned rest.

The conventional route to West Bay would begin from the car park at the bottom of the Beach Road that descends from the High Street in Charmouth, to make a direct ascent of Stonebarrow Hill from the wooden footbridge at the bottom of the car park. That possibility was, at the time of writing, unavailable following a long period of footpath closure due to landslips caused by several years of high rainfall. The nature of the geology on this stretch of the coastal footpath is, by its very nature, unstable. It would be wise therefore, to ready for route changes.

The importance of this footpath to the local communities ensures that the local authorities seek to reinstate or reroute paths with the minimum of delay and where diversions are made, they are well signposted. Few problems should be met therefore, provided the diversions are observed and you are not tempted, foolishly, to ignore them.

Until the original route is in some way reinstated, the way we must take to Stonebarrow Hill begins by walking east, towards Bridport, on the main road out of Charmouth town centre.

Shortly after crossing a bridge over the River Char, a smaller road (Stonebarrow Lane) turns half right from the main road. This road rises steeply and offers us our route to the summit where we can rejoin the coast path. This is a tedious climb. But at least height is quickly gained, and before long a cattle grid heralds the arrival of National Trust land and the summit.

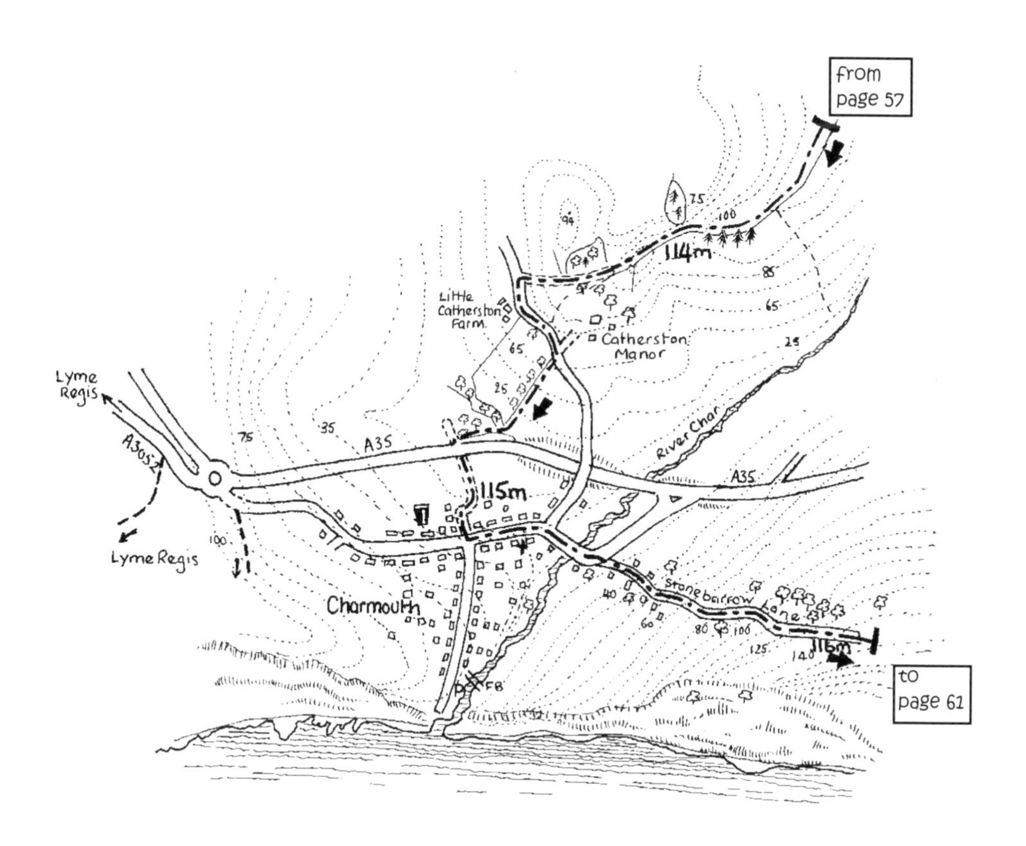

If the purist in you requires that Lyme Regis be included (as indeed it deserves to be), at the footbridge alongside the A35, turn north (right), on the Monarch's Way, and cross the open field ahead. Descend to the bottom right corner and pass through a metal gate and kissing gate then follow the fingerboard half left, to 'Thistle hill'. Through another metal gate turn half right and climb the slope towards the wooded area in the top corner. Here the footpath continues across the next field and to the left of its highest point. Through an opening there, continue ahead towards Hogchester Farm. The main route has been diverted and passes to the left of the farm buildings over a sequence of new stiles, after which we descend to the left to cross a foot bridge and there to ascend, once more to the A35 alongside some bungalows, a church and a cemetery.

Turn left to the roundabout. If the traditional coastal route has been reinstated this ascends to Timber hill from the minor road into Charmouth. Otherwise go up the A3052 and if the footpath across the Golf Course on Timber Hill is available then this can be used. The only other alternative is to follow the A3502 all the way into Lyme. This will I am afraid require you to retrace your steps tomorrow (a round trip of five or so miles) Negotiations are currently ongoing, and it is hoped that alternative routes will be opened across the golf course very shortly. (Phone 01305266920. – Dorset Countryside. Head Ranger.)

Charmouth to Burton Bradstock (9 miles)

After all the diversions it is good to finally stand at the start of this wonderful stretch of unspoilt coastline. Whether or not this is your first visit, you will not be disappointed. Provided you have checked that the gunnery ranges are going to be open, some of the most enjoyable walking and breathtaking views in England lie before you.

At the summit of Stonebarrow Hill, a well-established gravel track (the continuation of the coach road), along-side a parking area, runs along the top of the hill, past an information office, and is one of the many routes available off the hill towards Golden Cap, now a clear landmark. My elected route however is to go right, following the diversion signs as soon as the car park is reached.
Once through a gate (of the weave around type), at successive choices of way, keep turning to the left on grass paths until you pass through a gate once more heading east on a wider track.

This area is a maze of possible routes, none of which will lead you badly astray, but at the next fork, go right and begin to descend to a double farm track crossing from left to right. Turning right, almost back on yourself, descend the hill towards the farm below (Westhay Farm) passing a gate, stile and cattle grid on the way. The path passes the farm buildings on their left. Through a 'squeeze through' gate, continue to descend, with a sense of relief, to a cliff top track.

From this point on our walk around the perimeter of Dorset follows, for the most part, the Coastal Footpath. It is therefore very clearly way marked, and as a result route finding will not prove difficult and will thus render more detailed descriptions of the route rather superfluous.

Back on the Coastal Path. Towards Golden Cap.

More immediately, begin by heading down towards a solitary fingerboard in the direction of the cliff edge. It points us east towards Golden Cap and down to a footbridge, from where we climb, alongside a hedge, to another fingerboard and stile.

A flight of steps descends to a stream in a wooded dell, the first of three on the way to Golden Cap. As we approach the hill the route is clearly way marked around fields. Ahead, the path to the summit can just be discerned zigzagging its way up along a line of gorse bushes. A rope handrail has been provided to help pull you to pull yourself up.

When it is reached, the summit plateau is not as flat as it seemed, but is a collection of mounds or tumuli (two in fact, bronze age and dating from around 1600 BC). There is also a small stone monument dedicated to the Earl of Antrim KBE, Chairman of the National Trust 1966-1977. The route forward and the way off the summit are obvious. It turns away from the sea and after passing the trig point, descends to the North via steps. In the secluded valley below are the remains of the ancient settlement that surrounded the now ruined St Gabriel's Church.

After passing a gate a choice of routes can be made, but our chosen path turns to the right and continues to follow the designated Coastal Path on its way down into Seatown. The high wooded area to the north is Langdon Hill. Once again Coast Path diversion signs need to be observed, but few problems should be experienced.

Advanced notice of arrival at Seatown is provided in the form of rear gardens and a roadway. Turn to the right towards the pub (the Anchor), campsite and car park. It is fortunate, indeed propitious, that it is from here that the coastal path continues. The route itself is obvious as a grass track ascending Ridge Hill and Doghouse Hill, on its way to Thorncombe Beacon.

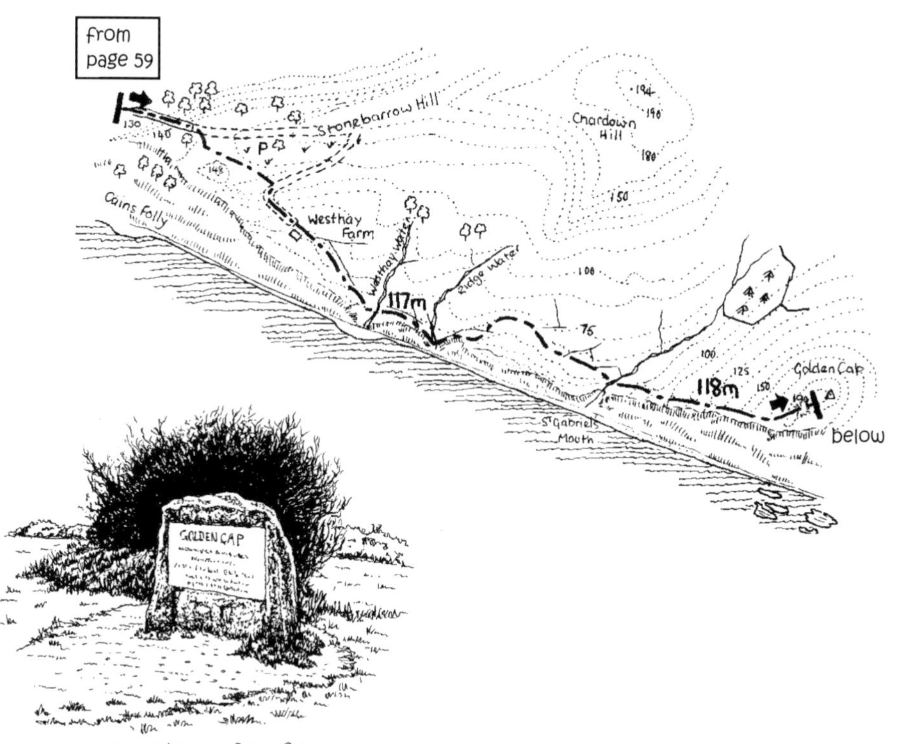

The Memorial Stone on Golden Cap.

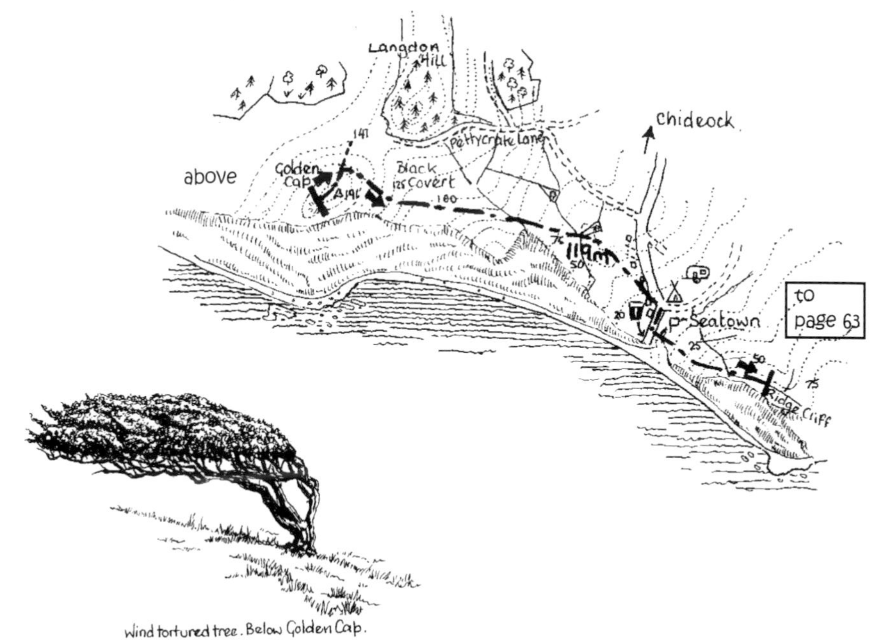

Wind tortured tree. Below Golden Cap.

Ridge Hill – Doghouse Hill – Thorncombe Beacon.

The walk to Thorncombe Beacon, and beyond to Eype Mouth and West Bay, is not as daunting as it looks. After climbing over Ridge Hill, the undulations are slight and the replica Armada Beacon Basket atop Thorncombe is an obvious target. As the beacon is approached, Colmer's Hill to the north, and Quarry Hill to its left, capture the attention.

Colmer's Hill is a clear landmark. Its conical form, crowned by the sculptured pines give it an oriental appearance as it overlooks the village of Symondsbury. If we had the time it would be hard to resist climbing it. It's that sort of hill.

On the descent from the beacon, in a field to the left is a circular stone-walled watering place for cattle. It has the appearance of a wellhead and will draw the curious to investigate. Eype Mouth (pronounced 'Eep') is spoiled by a plethora of holiday chalets and caravans but one must accept that it is a charming place if you do not favour solitude. A campsite and pub a quarter mile inland are available if time is short and the evening is drawing on.

Colmer's Hill

Descend to the shingle into which the Eype disappears, and cross by the footbridge or stepping-stones before ascending once more on the footpath to West Cliff. After passing another caravan site, begin to descend to the holiday centre of West Bay passing as you do an old coast guard lookout station (now a home).

Here is accommodation and distractions in plenty, both in West Bay and its larger neighbour, Bridport. (Rope making and shipbuilding were the principle industries of Bridport. The ropes were used in many ships, but also to provide the wherewithal for what was Britain's chosen method of capital punishment. To be hanged was referred to as being 'stabbed with a Bridport dagger'.)

The large building that dominates West Bay and incorporates the Bay House Hotel is Pier Terrace, known locally as 'Noah's Ark'.

We leave West Bay by walking past Pier Terrace and the Bridport Arms Hotel to the beach then turning left towards East Cliff. East Cliff is the first of a series of vertical cliffs revealing clear banding that will be invisible to us as we climb them. Instead our attention will most likely be drawn to the golf course that lines the top. Now this is what I call a water hazard.

"Noah's Ark". West Bay

Without any real problems and a few minor undulations, continue along the cliff top and after a mile or so, descend with the path, to Burton Freshwater. Here there is a large holiday camp and a stream to be crossed (The River Bride). The stream disappears in to the shingle, but turn left and walk along its western bank, on the grass, towards Burton Bradstock . Walk around the northern side of the high ground of Burton Cliff until a stile leads to a small footbridge. Over this, we could slavishly follow the coastal footpath by walking to the right, and some may elect to do so, instead, turn left along the path, and follow the stream, on low ground, towards Southover at the southern end of the village of Burton Bradstock.

After passing into a lane, an ivy-covered fingerboard (well it was in 2004) offers a route to the right (south) back up onto the cliff top. Take this route to rejoin the coastal path above Burton Beach.

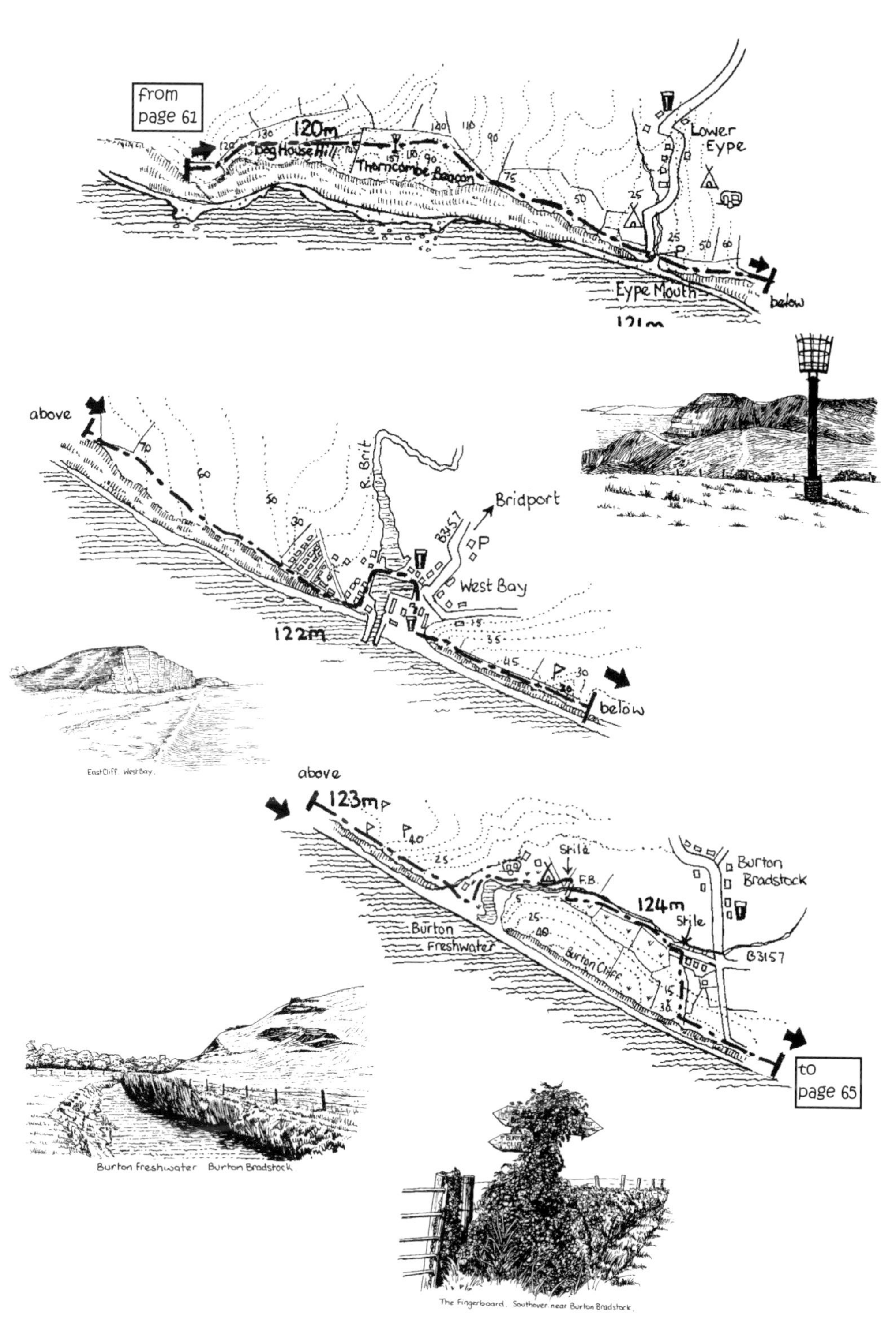

East Cliff West Bay.

Burton Freshwater Burton Bradstock

The Fingerboard, Southover near Burton Bradstock.

Burton Bradstock – Upwey (15½ miles)

When the coastal path is rejoined above Burton Beach, continue down to the holiday homes, and then up again alongside, and below, the summit of Bind Barrow. Beyond the old coastguard house and caravan site, the path continues more clearly as it descends to Cogden Beach. Here begins a low level walk either on or alongside the shingle (the precursor of Chesil bank) towards Burton Mere.

There are two routes around the mere, one on the landward side of it, and the other on the shingle bank itself. Unless the landward route is unusable because of flooding, go that way and avoid the additional effort required to walk on the pebbles (now is not the time for heroics). The route to West Bexington, one mile further on, is clear and follows the fence line for much of the way.

Reed beds in this area justify its classification as a nature reserve and should be respected. Looking inland on the skyline is a conspicuous hill known as 'The Knoll', the lonely building at its summit being an old coastal lookout station.

West Bexington is met at a car park and café alongside the shingle bank. A cup of tea is recommended at this point for it is here that we depart from the coastline to take the inland route along the ridge way. (Further refreshment can only be found by descending to a village, accepting as you do, the re-ascent that follows.) However, this section is well worth the additional effort, it will linger in the memory as a high point.

Unparalleled views in all directions are the rewards of ridge walking and this is a wonderful ridge. The walking is easy and the underfoot conditions ideal. Route finding is straightforward and all around are archaeological, geological and historical features to add to the overall interest.

That first effort begins by turning left on to the tarmac road leading away from the beach. The road rises steadily between houses, those on the left, particularly, enjoying wonderful views back towards Golden Cap. After ¼ mile the road turns to the left alongside a private hotel. A rocky track, straight ahead and alongside a house should be taken to continue directly up the hill towards the B3157.

Before reaching the roadway, turn half right along a sidetrack with a fingerboard pointing the way to the Hardy monument. In a short while you will emerge onto the B3157, the road between Bridport and Abbotsbury. It is a busy road especially on high days and holidays, and for those confined to four wheels, it is a road to be enjoyed for the views it offers, but our route is even better.

Tulk's Hill.

The stile approaching the B3157. Below Abbotsbury Castle. The Fleet and Portland beyond.

Turn to the right and almost immediately, leave the road by taking the signed footpath heading half right. This area is called Limekiln Hill, and justification for the name comes soon after as the path, following the line of a thorn hedge, heads back to the road and passes a restored limekiln. The deep shaft has a spring emerging at its base.

The path runs parallel to the road and around the edge of a meadow, on its seaward side, passing at one point an elevated pond surrounded by thorn bushes. Continue ahead rising gently past a lesser tumulus with a more significant one ahead. This turns out to be a pair of tumuli. The path continues to rise to a dry-stone wall and leads to a stile in a corner that gives access, once more, to the roadway.

Linger a while and take in the view to the south east, towards Chesil Bank and the Fleet, and the Isle of Portland.

The true coastal path continues from West Bexington towards Abbotsbury and then follows the Fleet to Portland before turning into Weymouth. This is itself an interesting route. Often scenic, it would be in all other circumstances, an excellent day's walk. It also facilitates an additional and truly delightful walk around the coastal path of Portland itself. However, the alternative I recommend is finer in all respects for those who, like me, prefer their walking on higher, more open ground, and away from the crowds and urban sprawl.

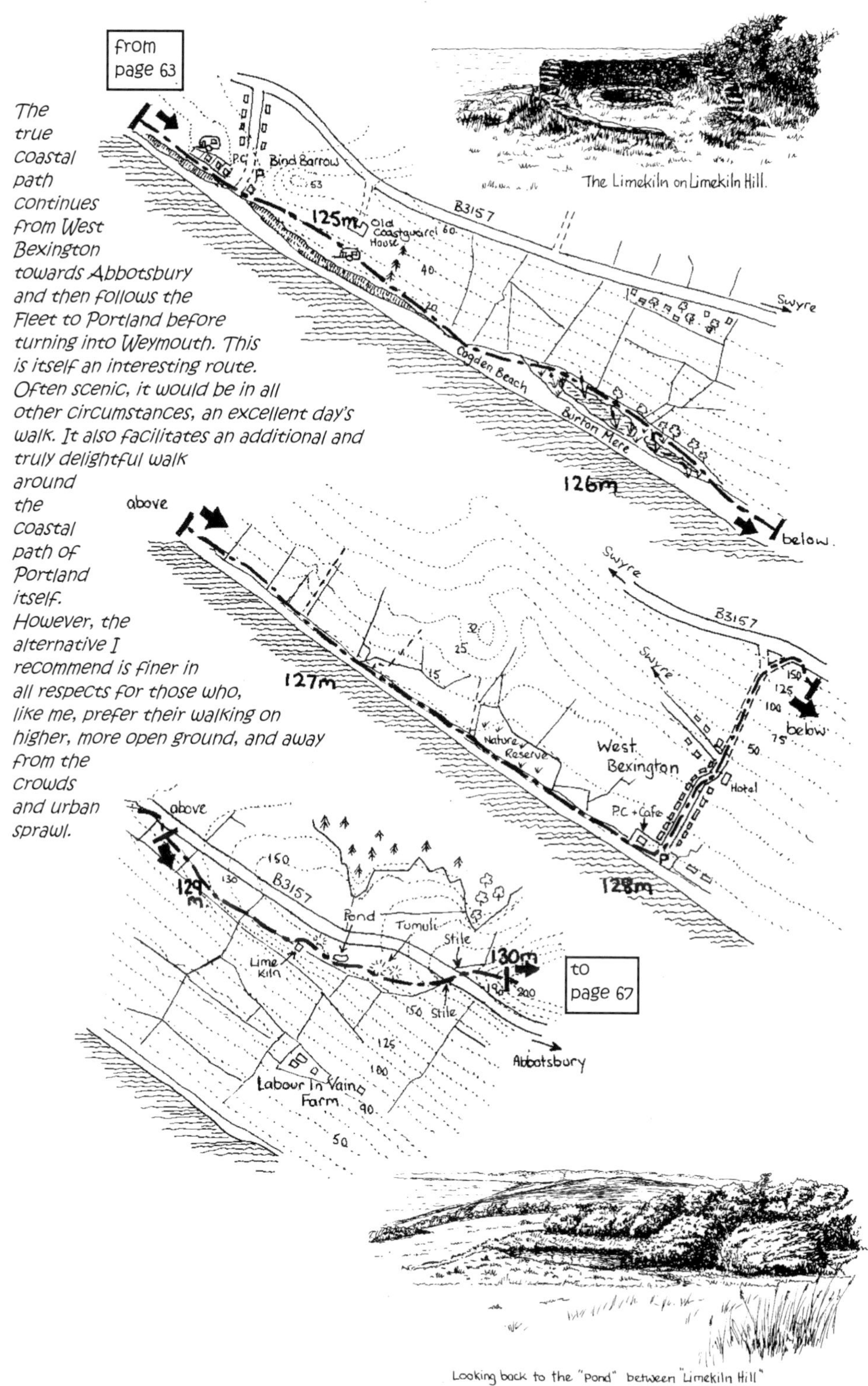

The Limekiln on Limekiln Hill.

Looking back to the "Pond" between "Limekiln Hill" and "Tulk's Hill".

To the west, and ahead of us, is the higher ground of Abbotsbury Castle and the beginning of the high ridge way that will take us around Weymouth towards Osmington. Looking further to high ground beyond, we get our first glimpse of the Hardy Monument on the skyline.

Over the stile, cross the road to a stile on the other side and beyond it to the grassy slope up to the summit of Abbotsbury Castle, yet another Iron Age hill fort, (busy people these Durotriges). Aim to the right of the summit tumulus and by the time you reach the trig point, if you haven't done so already, you will need to stand and take in the breathtaking beauty that surrounds you. This is a wonderful place.
It is worth mentioning the tumuli on this stretch of the walk. Between here and Osmington they will be seen in amazing numbers, and surely nowhere else in the U.K. can they be seen in such abundance. They stand in ancient witness to the significance attached to this ridge by its early occupants.

In lovely surroundings, with views in every direction one really gets an impression of the character of Dorset with its coastline and rolling hills stretching out before you. The route crosses the earthworks of Abbotsbury Castle and soon passes the trig point and across a very minor road that crosses the ridge and serves some remote farms on its northern side. The Hardy Monument, ever a feature of the Dorset coast, now stands more clearly as our next goal, not that you will want to hurry the next few miles, the walking is unparalleled, you will enjoy it.

The route heads clearly up to Wears Hill passing another tumulus. If the walking could get easier it does so beyond a small, partially ruined small brick building and what looks like a wellhead. (The craggy headland on the coast ahead, to the left of Weymouth, is White Nothe, a feature with which we shall have a closer acquaintance in a day or two.) On a grassy ridge, the route turns slightly left and begins its arc around Abbotsbury. St Catherine's Chapel, standing on its solitary hill is a key feature of this village. With the availability of refreshment and accommodation, Abbotsbury may well be the chosen destination for tonight. It is certainly worth a diversion.

St Catherine's Chapel

The path descends slightly towards some limestone outcrops and, down to the right, it passes an area of wet ground surrounded by hides. If Abbotsbury is your immediate destination, it is beyond here (past an old quarry that would make an ideal bivouac) that your path drops down to the village and will be your point of ascent in the morning. Otherwise, continue along the ridge.

A gate on the ridge above Abbotsbury has, in attendance, a fingerboard showing the way to the Hardy Monument in three miles. Through another metal gate we continue along the ridge soon to be joined by a barbed wire fence. Beyond a gate in a corner, the fence line switches to our right and soon begins to descend, half left, to a roadway alongside a bend. (Bishop's Road)

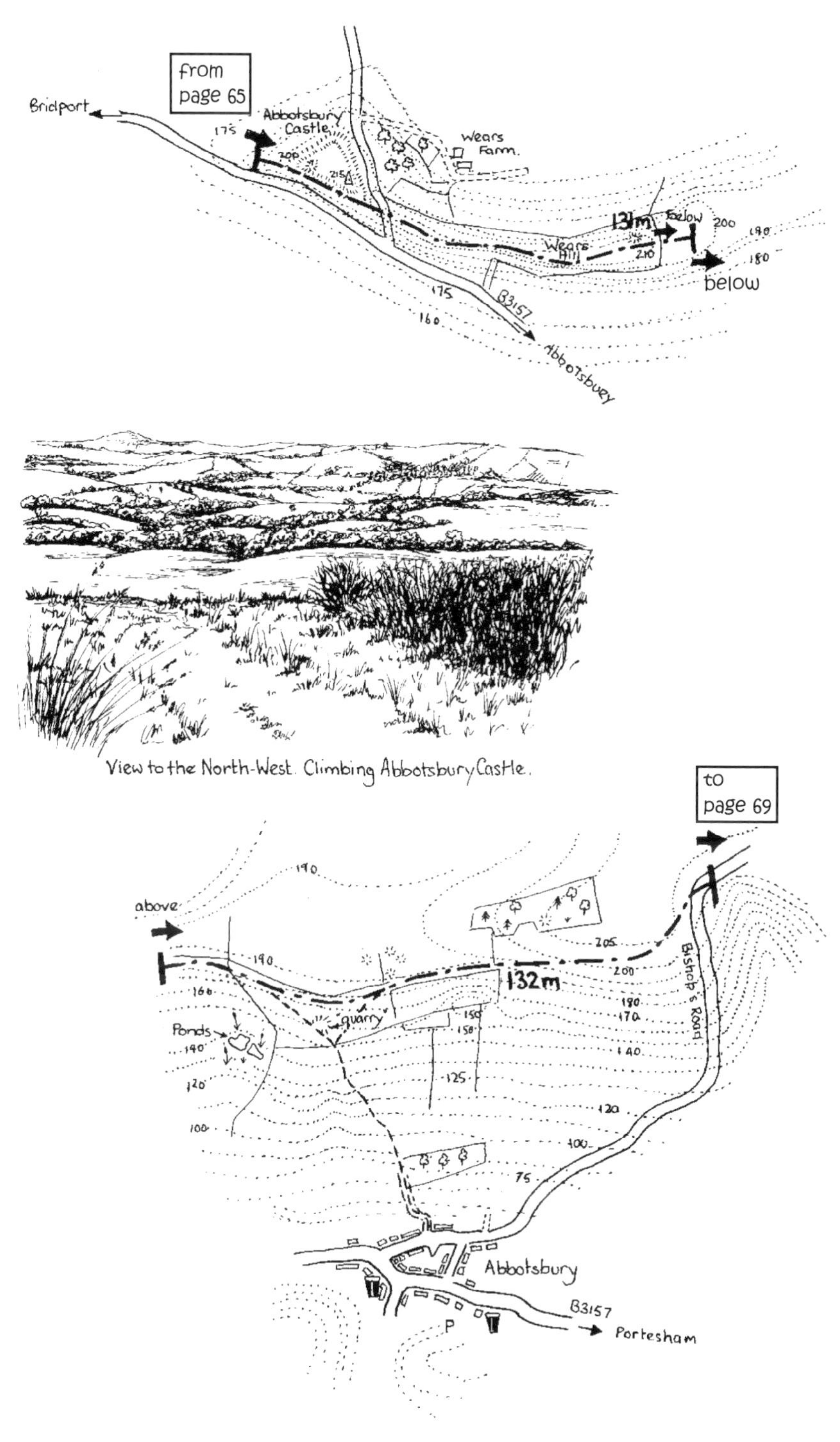

View to the North-West. Climbing Abbotsbury Castle.

Turn initially left to a path on the right. In 40 or so paces a gate and fingerboard lead on to a narrow path contouring around a deep valley falling away to the right. The fence line should be on our left with extensive views to the coast and the area around Weymouth across the valley.

At a fork in the path alongside a way-stone, take the left fork still heading towards the monument. Beyond a stile and gate, the path, now bearing the mark of tractor wheels, begins to descend to the trees surrounding the farm buildings associated with Hampton Barn. This in turn leads to the 'B' road crossing the summit of 'Portesham Hill'. Camping is available 1 mile south down the road in Portesham village.

At the road, encouraged by a signpost to the inland route, turn to the left and in a few yards turn right at a stile in a hedgerow. Follow the line of the fence along the top of a field. The Hardy Monument, half left, at last seems to be drawing closer. The area of forestry land beneath it now becomes evident. (On my last two visits, electric fencing, an increasing and unwelcome hindrance, has obstructed these fields.) Continue along the top of the field 'limbo-ing' or hurdling the electric fencing. Two stiles confirm the right of way along the top of these fields as we descend to the corner of Benecke Wood. At the bottom of the field, alongside the wood, cross two stiles (the second made of stone).

The path turns initially half right to skirt the bottom of the wood. At a clear footpath entering the wood and climbing Black Down, turn to the left and begin the ascent on a forest track towards The Hardy Monument.
The route of ascent is clear apart from a fork in a ¼ mile at which the clearer right fork is taken. Shortly after, the track emerges into an area of gorse and scrub with the towering monument ahead and half right. Choose your route to it.

At 770 feet above sea level and commanding a view across to the Port of Weymouth and The Isle of Portland, this 70ft tower commemorates the life of Vice Admiral Sir Thomas Masterman Hardy, the officer who shared the deck of the Victory with Nelson at Trafalgar and to whom the immortal last words 'kiss me Hardy' were uttered. (Not Thomas Hardy the Dorset author). The monument was erected in 1844, five years after Hardy's death. It is a little over a mile from his family home in Portesham.

When you are ready to leave the summit of Black Down, go down to the road running alongside the monument and descend, on the road, to the right. (A short footpath leaving the road on the left cuts off the next short section of road but was overgrown at the time of writing and hardly seemed worth the effort). The road descends steeply and after a hundred yards, a second fingerboard on the right indicates the continuation of the inland coastal path. Turn here, initially southeast, on to a clear gravel track above the attractive valley of Hell's Bottom and in so doing, once more on to the ridge way and the joyous walking it affords.

Hardy's Monument

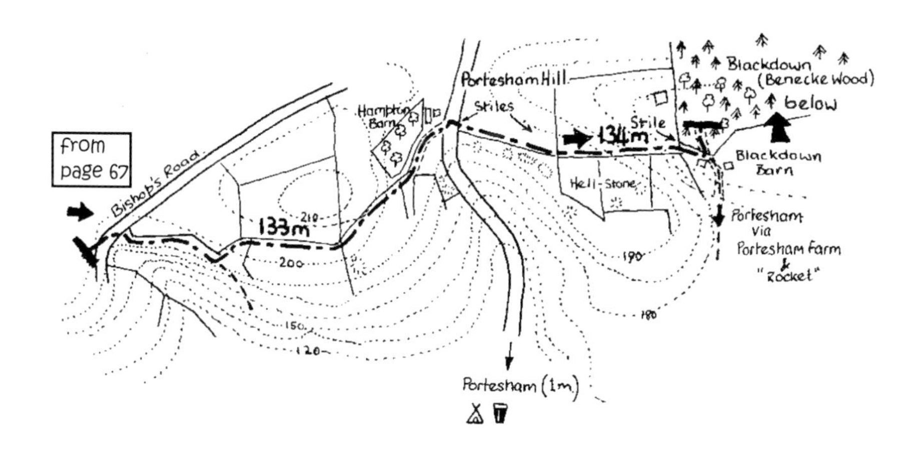

From the stone stile on Portesham Hill, a permissive path crosses the neighbouring field on a diagonal (half left), to the Hell Stone, a 19th Century reconstruction of a chambered Stone Age barrow. If the path can be found (it is not obvious), and the time is available, it may be an interesting diversion.

Hellstone Dolmen. Near Portesham.

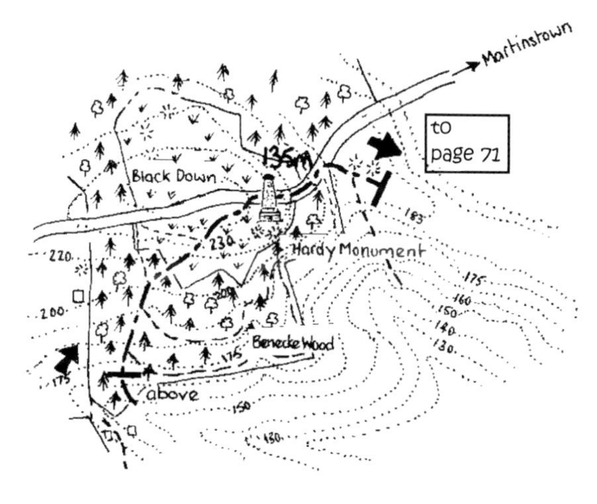

The ancient track continues clearly ahead with no navigational difficulties as it passes through a series of gates across Bronkham Hill, passing as it does a path to the left towards Martinstown.

The early part of this stretch of ridge way provides a rich sense of ancient history. The many wonderfully preserved tumuli close to the left and the sunken areas around them known as 'shake holes' will not fail to grab your attention (I have not as yet managed to find the cause or true nature of these features). This earlier section is alongside a fence, often with an old but beautifully crafted dry stone wall to the right. At one point, where this wall ends, what appears to be stone paving slabs have been turned on their edge to serve as a border to the path.

Beyond the walled track, and the initial profusion of tumuli, the main track continues ahead through an area of gorse scrub before descending to pass farming paraphernalia and a path off to the right towards Coryates. Continue on ahead passing in turn earthworks , a farm track to the left, and a sequence of overhead power lines providing electricity to meet the demands of the people of Weymouth. The town is in view but seems a world and many centuries away.

A Tumulus on the ridge way
East of Bronkham Hill and North of Friar Waddon

If the route could get any clearer, it does so now, and apart from rounding between two tumuli (in three gates time) that obstruct the line of walking (see illustration), no problems will be met for the next two miles. A small mast sighted on the ridge, is our next target.

Along this section eyes will be increasingly drawn to the North east and the area surrounding the ancient capital of Dorset, Dorchester, (Durnovaria to the Romans). As we approach the higher ground of Ridge Hill, earthworks (that are the rings and ditches of Maiden Castle) should be visible between you and the sprawl of the town of Dorchester. It is interesting to consider the significance of all the tumuli that characterise this ridge, to the ancients occupying Maiden Castle so many years ago. Being higher than they are today, they must have been an awesome sight lining the high ground above their homes. Silhouetted against the setting sun, they would make a clear statement of the rank of those buried there and the power of the tribe that constructed them.
If you have time to turn away to explore Maiden Castle or have accommodation off route in Martinstown or Dorchester, the path towards Higher Ashton Farm affords an ideal opportunity to do so.

Beyond the mast and its surrounding compound, descend to the B3159 and cross it to the continuation of the ridge. In a short ¼ mile, beyond yet more tumuli, an attractive valley dropping away to the right provides the preferred route to Upwey, and a potential overnight stop. If the time of day and your fitness is not a problem however, continue ahead before descending towards the busy A354 from Weymouth to Dorchester (½ mile). As you approach the road turn to the right on a track that descends parallel with the main road. In approximately ¼ mile look for a stile in the hedgerow on the left. It will lead us across a long, but narrow field to the road itself. This is our crossing point and where we rejoin those who have come from the village.

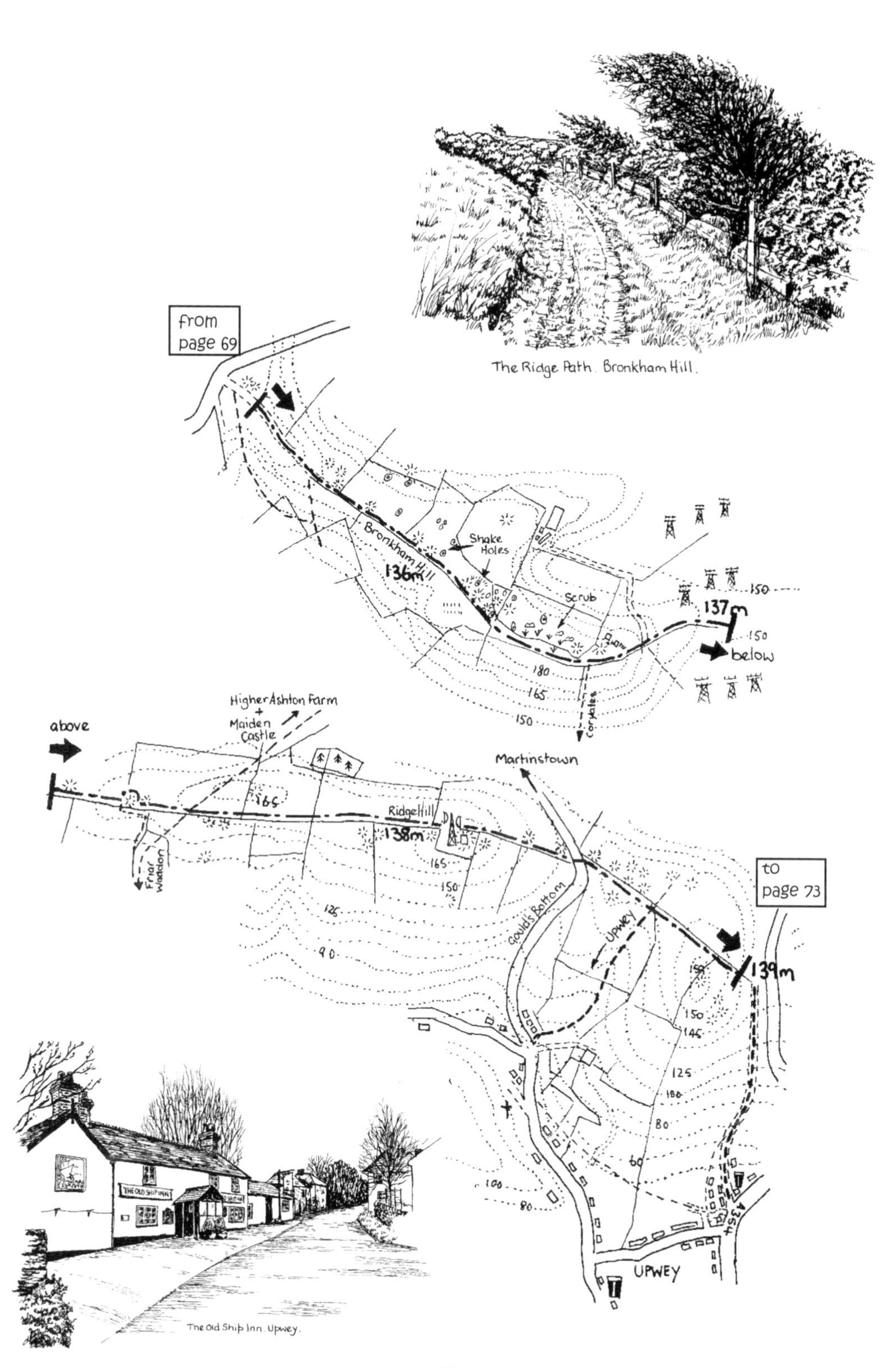

The Ridge Path. Bronkham Hill.

The Old Ship Inn. Upwey.

Upwey to Lulworth Cove (12 Miles)

If you have rested in the village of Upwey, leave via the lane that passes in front of the Old Ship Inn (Tel: 01305 812522). Initially on tarmac and alongside cottages, it soon deteriorates and continues as a rocky track that climbs parallel to the A354. In a ¼ mile, after crossing a farm track, look for a stile in the hedgerow on the right, go over this and head to the road. Cross the road with care, where we join the main route, and there go through a gate to a right of way. The slightly sunken path climbs alongside a fence and scanty hedgerow toward a ridge on your left and arrives at a gate just below a communications mast. Do not turn up towards the mast, but continue ahead through a gate towards another gate in the far corner of the field, and a third gate beyond that one. Follow the fence line below two tumuli and along the bottom of a field that soon turns up to meet a minor road opposite a golf course. Turn to the right and walk down the road to where it is met by another road from the left, coming from Dorchester. At this point turn right on a farm track that heads south to the village of Bincombe ¾ mile ahead. This track descends gently with occasional views to the southwest back towards Upwey.

The gate "just below a Communication mast". Bincombe Down.

The track meets a metalled surface from a mast on the left. Continue ahead down towards the farm buildings and the cottages now in sight. At the junction turn to the left and descend to the village itself. At a bend in the road continue ahead on a farm road between a high wall and old barns. Beyond the wall, we pass Holy Trinity Church, a partially Norman structure that seems to have grown out of the soil on which it stands. Bincombe claims associations with Thomas Hardy but more illustriously, claims to be the location in which the celebrated Grand Old Duke Of York marched his men to the top of the hill, then marched them down again. It seems these were men of the York Hussars who were camped here at the beginning of the 19th century. (The Duke was the brother of King George III, with whom we will soon establish a more intimate acquaintance.)

Middle Farm. Bincombe.

In truly delightful surroundings, the lane from the church begins to turn to the right. Here turn left on to the path that climbs alongside the terraced side of Bincombe Hill. The path soon becomes a ledge traversing the side of the hill towards a pylon at the head of the small valley. (The pylon is a blot on an otherwise lovely landscape that you will have to try to 'filter it out'.)

The view over the head of the valley (or coombe) will not disappoint you. Like crossing a hause in the Lake Dstrict, a whole new vista opens up. On the horizon stands the coastal headland of White Nothe, and between lays the village of Osmington, both on our route 'Round Dorset'.

Head a ¼ left to a single gate in a dry-stone-wall beneath the overhead cables. Follow the top of the field to another gate in the not-so-far corner. From here take the path that descends to the left, towards the bend in the road, snaking through 'Coombe Valley'.

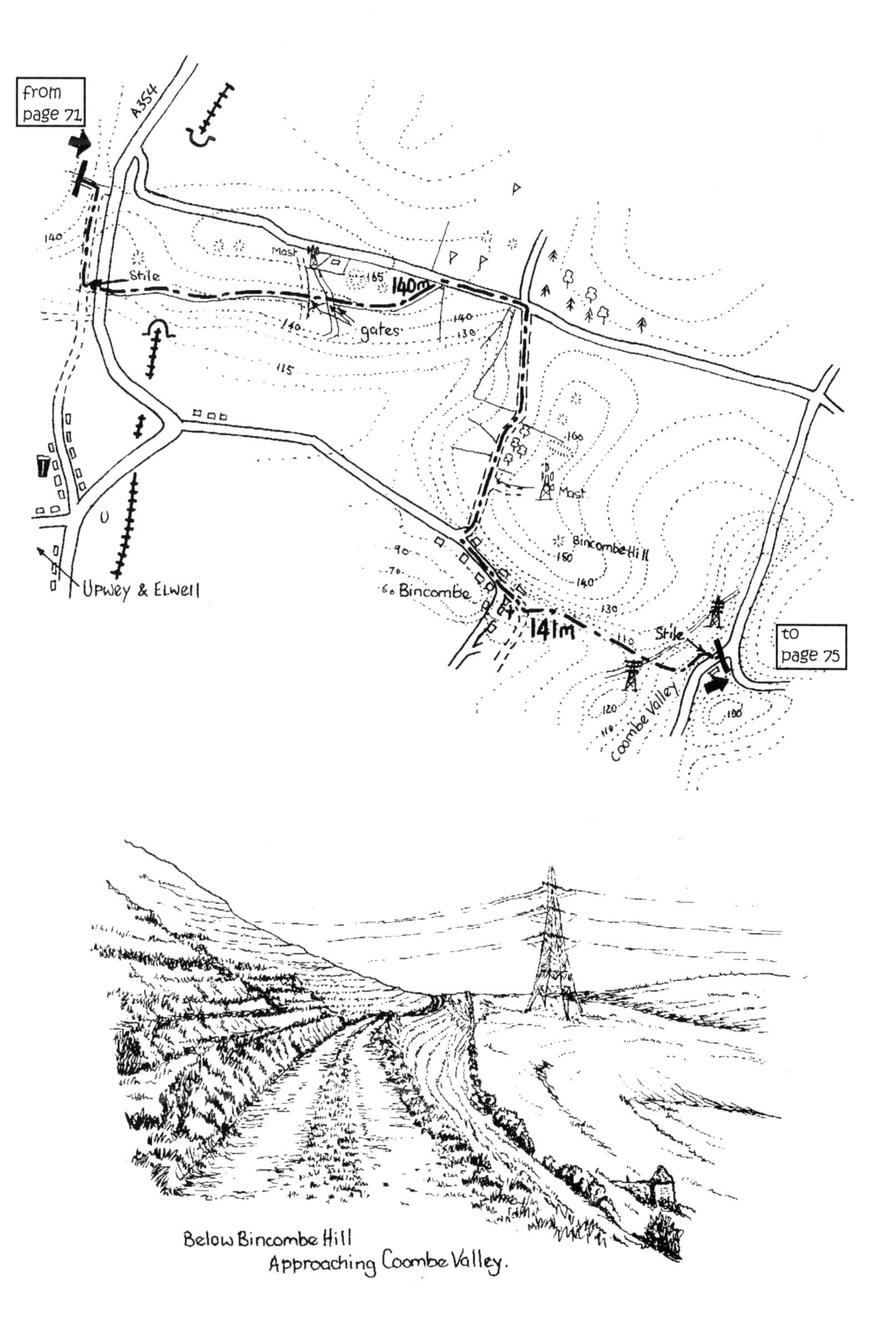

Below Bincombe Hill
Approaching Coombe Valley.

West Hill. Above Spring Bottom and Sutton Poyntz.

At the roadside cross the stile to the road and turn left to walk past the disused farm buildings. At the next bend in the road, take the lane on the right up towards a fingerboard. Through the gate on the left, we start to gently ascend the hill once more. Beyond the next gate, keep the fence line on your left and continue ahead. The path now begins to round the top of the valley of Spring Bottom. (Accommodation and a pub -the 'Springhead'- can be found below in Sutton Poyntz)

Walk to the head of the valley between two tumuli and, if you are not looking for accommodation, avoid the diagonal track descending right. Join the main path between fences, towards the high ground and the prominent tumulus on the skyline. After passing the trig point in the field to the right, at the next gate a permissive route gives access to the White Horse carved into the hillside. It seems churlish to get this far and not to pay your respects, so make a detour and turn to the right, round a tumulus (another one!), and go down to meet King George III and his horse. I said we would meet him again! Your initial encounter will most probably be with his bicorne hat. (Note the clever way the maker allowed for the foreshortening effect of the curvature of the hill.)

Having traced his outline (avoiding damage to the fragile carving by not walking on it), turn back and retrace your steps to the fence at the top of the field, and there turn right to the gate in the next corner. Beyond this turn half right onto a clear chalk track, to descend to the valley below and the village of Osmington. In approximately 1 mile the track arrives at a tarmac road through the village. Turn around here and inspect the horse as it was meant to be viewed.

Looking back from the lane into Osmington.

Walk up the narrow street alongside renovated cottages, a church, and a disused village pump to the junction with the very busy A353 carrying holiday traffic to Weymouth. Without delay turn left and head past the Sunray pub. Cross the road and after about 200 yards, when beyond 'Craigs Farm Dairy', look for a small footpath on the right that descends to a footbridge over a ditch, to a stile into a field.

Climb the field to the stile in the top left corner. Over this, stay to the left and head to the next stile which is not quite in the next corner. Once at the crest of the small ridge, descend the field ahead in the direction of a pole carrying a power line, and so to the stile in the fence beyond it. The hamlet of Osmington Mills is ahead, set against the sea. Once over the stile continue to keep the hedgerow on your left, over which can be seen the camp site that dominates the area and might afford an overnight stop for those of you carrying tents or whatever. Across the next stile, a wooden walkway gives access to a narrow path and steps that descend to the roadway to the coast. (The camp shop, where refreshments can be purchased, and reception are to the left.)

Turn right and continue down the road to the car park that overlooks The Smuggler's Inn and heralds our return to the coastal footpath.

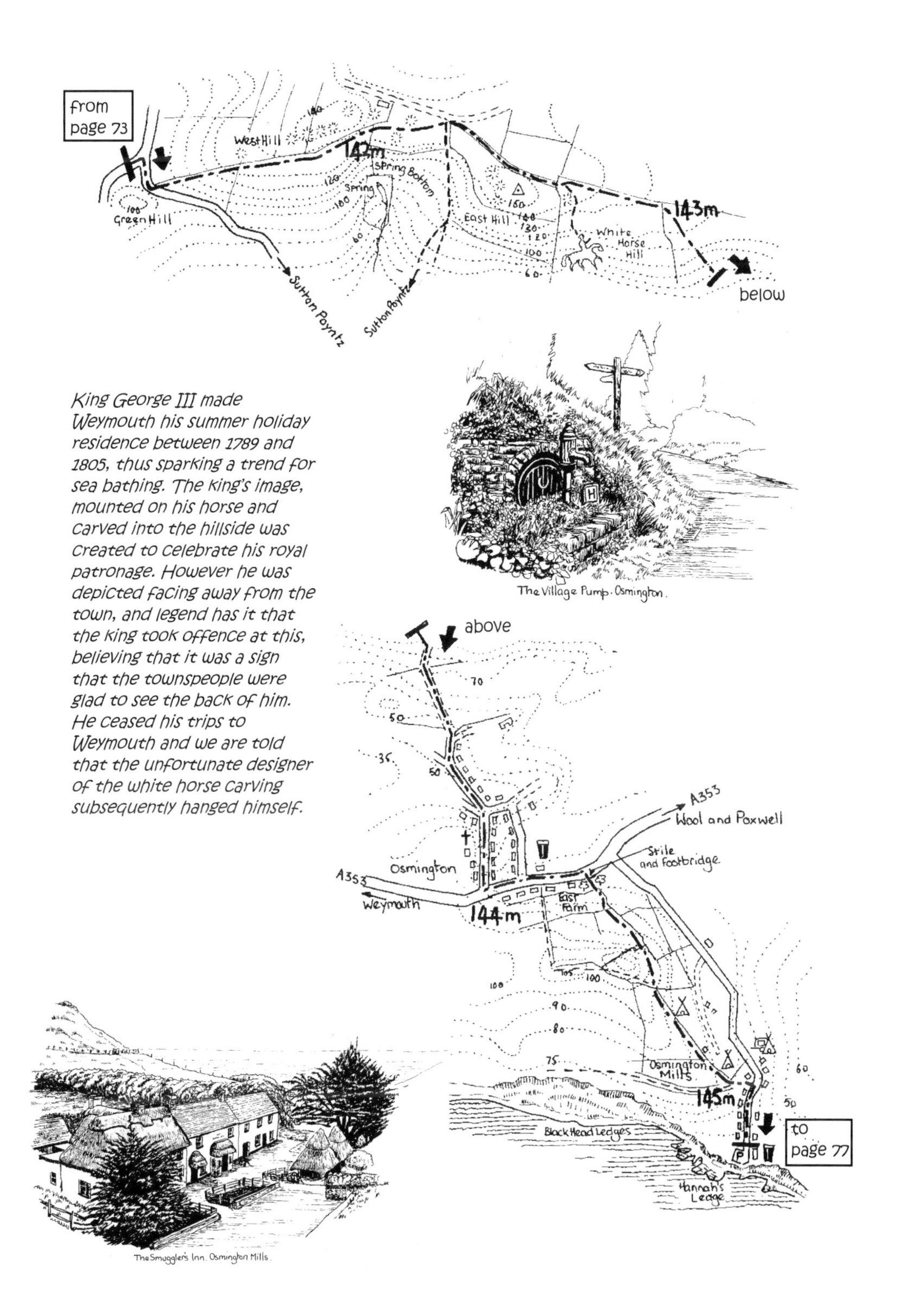

King George III made Weymouth his summer holiday residence between 1789 and 1805, thus sparking a trend for sea bathing. The king's image, mounted on his horse and carved into the hillside was created to celebrate his royal patronage. However he was depicted facing away from the town, and legend has it that the king took offence at this, believing that it was a sign that the townspeople were glad to see the back of him. He ceased his trips to Weymouth and we are told that the unfortunate designer of the white horse carving subsequently hanged himself.

The Village Pump. Osmington.

The Smuggler's Inn. Osmington Mills.

If the temptation to linger a while in the comforts of the 'Smugglers' is hard to resist, it will not help you to know that you must descend the flight of steps to the front door of the pub before passing round the building to the left. Here a path leads between the pub and a the gardens of a row of cottages, to a 'kissing gate'. Once through the gate avoid the path to the beach on the right, and continue ahead to another kissing gate and a path that ascends the hill, beside a fence, towards a tangle of blackthorn.

The path continues through the bushes and emerges on the cliff edge overlooking Hannah's Ledge.

The path on the seaward side of the fence descends to an area of bushes and stunted trees at Bran Point. Beyond Bran Point descend steeply into a wooded dell and cross a footbridge over a stream flowing from its source in Spring Bottom to the sea just twenty yards away.

Steps on the far side of the stream lead to a continuation of the path, and a short walk to the cottages of Ringstead. The path passes the cottages and turns left to a café and shop which sells just about everything from a tent to a cup of tea and a slice of fine Dorset Apple cake.

The route out of Ringstead towards the headland of White Nothe (O.E 'nose'), is to the seaward side of the café, between the semi-permanent toilet block and a row of cottages and holiday homes.

It is a broad gravel track that begins its ascent after passing an open area on the right. Here the path narrows as it enters low woodland beneath overhanging blackthorn.

White Nothe.

On emerging from the wooded area, continue to cimb alongside the ciff edge towards the cottages and church that overlook Burning Cliff. (This was formed by a landslip in the early 19th century after which the organically rich clay, exposed to the air, began to smoulder, and went on doing so for four years). The church, (St Catherines By The Sea) is a small wooden buiding; more of a chapel really. Its surroundings are idyllic.

Just beyond the church the metalled surface begins to turn to the left. At this point leave the road at a stile and continue ahead alongside the fence. At the track to Holworth House, cross to the stile and begin to climb the hill on a path, ½ right, through the gorse. Once out of the gorse, a stile at the summit serves as your immediate target. From the stile retrospective views to the west and towards Portland and Weymouth are worth dwelling on. To the east, the coast guard cottages on the summit of White Nothe beckon, and the walk to them is straight-forward.

Around a ¼ mile beyond the cottages, at the point at which the path overlooks West Bottom and The Warren, a view opens up that on a fine day will dwell in the memory. A stretch of coastline is revealed that is at once peaceful and dramatic and in many ways defines the Dorset Coast. The first headland is that of Bat's Head with its small natural arch, and beyond that Swyre Head. Durdle Door and its more famous rock formation can just be glimpsed behind Swyre Head. The two rocks in the sea off Bat's Head, are called the 'cow' and the 'calf' and look for all the world like surfacing whales (female and young presumably).

Sit awhile and enjoy it.

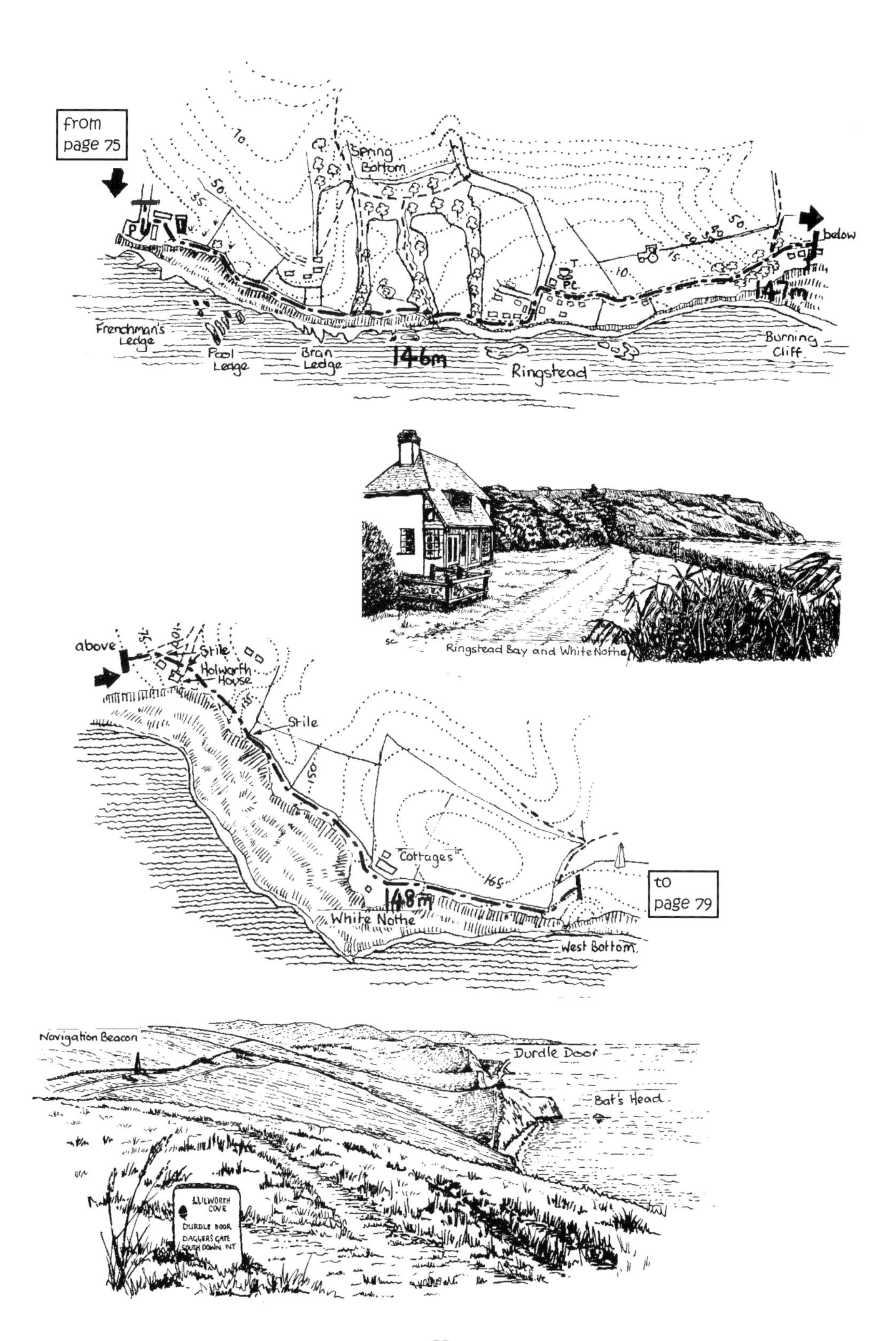

Ringstead Bay and White Nothe

Follow the narrow path as it curves around West Bottom. After it passes a navigational column the path begins the steepening descent to Middle Bottom, almost at sea level. From Middle Bottom begins the first of two severe climbs and more severe descents crossing Bat's Head and Swyre Head to Scratchy Bottom.

"Middle Bottom".

Swyre Head

It is from this final descent that Durdle Door and its almost iconic arch can most be enjoyed. From here to our ascent of Hambury Tout, the arch and its bay will dominate our attention. ('Durdle' is a corruption of the old English word 'thirl', meaning 'holed'. In the Dorset dialect 'th' is pronounced 'd'.)

A path runs from Scratchy Bottom to the camp site at Newland's Farm (Durdle Door Caravan and Camp site) if that is your target. It can be reached equally easily from paths that turn inland from Lulworth or the summit of Hambury Tout, and it seems pointless to miss out on one of the landmarks of the walk when so close. Instead, climb the path that follows the bay to inspect the 'Door' at closer quarters.

This is a popular tourist attraction and will seem hectic after the peace of the previous miles, but is an area well worth exploring if time and energy are to spare.

Durdle Door

From Durdle Door it is tempting to follow the main track as it turns inland around Hambury Tout (the high ground ahead), but beyond the tea caravan and the path down to Man o' War Cove and Oswald's Bay, continue ahead on the lesser track ascending Hambury Tout (see p.83 for meaning of 'tout').

From the summit, a well made track descends to Lulworth Cove and the vast car parks below. Here you will find cafes, fish and chips, gift shops, and a host of students wearing hard hats, Lulworth is a Geologist's classroom. Its unique features are required study, and feature in a host of text books. (The perfectly formed circular cove and its younger sibling Stair Hole, and their formation, are described in a display in the Heritage Centre. It is well worth a visit).

Man O'War Cove.

Accommodation can be found inland on the B3070 at West Lulworth. This could include the Youth Hostel and the worthy Castle Inn (01929 400 311).

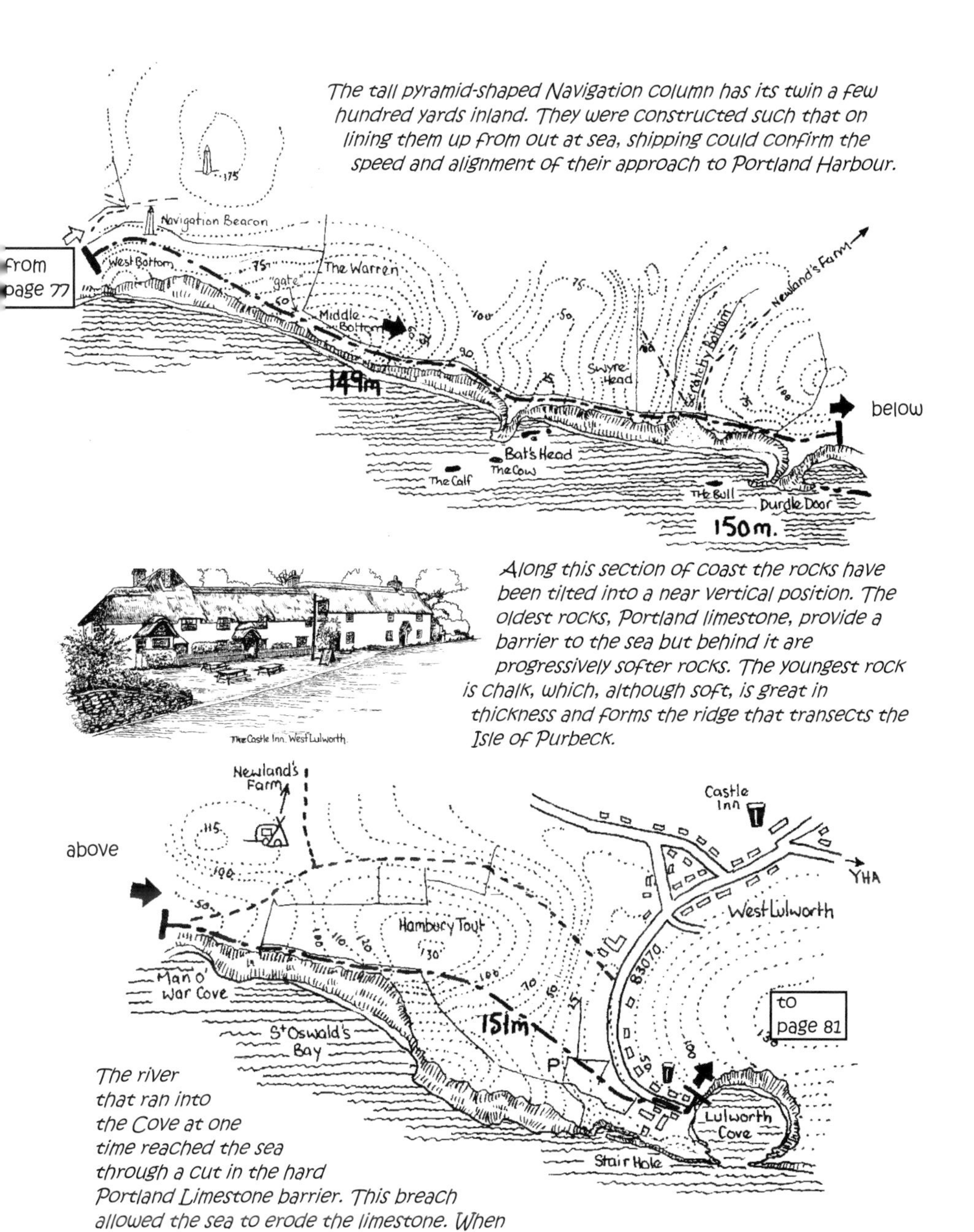

The tall pyramid-shaped Navigation column has its twin a few hundred yards inland. They were constructed such that on lining them up from out at sea, shipping could confirm the speed and alignment of their approach to Portland Harbour.

The Castle Inn, West Lulworth

Along this section of coast the rocks have been tilted into a near vertical position. The oldest rocks, Portland limestone, provide a barrier to the sea but behind it are progressively softer rocks. The youngest rock is chalk, which, although soft, is great in thickness and forms the ridge that transects the Isle of Purbeck.

The river that ran into the Cove at one time reached the sea through a cut in the hard Portland Limestone barrier. This breach allowed the sea to erode the limestone. When the sea reached the softer rocks behind the limestone rapid erosion took place. Once the sea reached the massive chalk ridge, erosion slowed, forming the perfect bay. To the west, the sea has been eroding the Portland Limestone at Stair Hole. Eventually Lulworth Cove and Stair Hole will combine into one larger cove.

Durdle Door also formed as a result of the softer rocks being eroded away behind the hard limestone. The action of the sea has created the arch and will eventually cause it to collapse and so leave a 'sea stack' like other pinnacles and jagged teeth that line this coast.

Lulworth Cove To Corfe Castle. (9½ miles.)

The section from Lulworth to Creech Hill, on the Purbeck ridgeway, enters the military gunnery ranges that restrict access to the coastal footpath for much of the year. You were warned, so hopefully you will have done your homework and timed your arrival to coincide with the weekend, or the days of free access. If so, leave Lulworth by walking down to the cove itself, past the Cove Inn and the duck pond.

Just before the beach turn left up a flight of steps. Height is gained rapidly to 125m, so I shall say no more other than that you may choose to have a short rest at the stile that concludes the climb.

Once over the stile, turn immediately right to follow the fence-line back towards the sea. The 'scrub' on your right soon clears to permit increasingly rewarding views down to the cove below and along the coast towards St Aldhem's Head.

Looking back to Lulworth Cove.

At a stone way-marker you have a choice, to turn up to the summit of Binden Hill (Radar Hill), or to continue on to the lower headland of Little Binden. The upper route is easier and shorter, but misses out on the 'unmissable'. It's worth the effort, so follow me.

There are two routes down to Little Binden, so follow the way-markers. The second turns to the right as the fence line turns up the hill. Here begins a steep descent on steps around the Cove (a good place for retrospective photographs).

When the descent finally eases, do not go down to the beach, but turn inland to go around the 'cut', and from there to climb back to the headland that is the eastern lip of Lulworth Cove (Little Bindon).

The path now heads to the east and into the gunnery ranges via an intimidating fence and gate adorned with warning signs and restrictions.

The Fossil Forest is a short climb down from the coastal path (and back to it!). It is an extra effort on a day that will not be short of effort, but it would be a shame to miss it. Step back a few million years; it's a world apart down there.

The path continues above the 'forest', and some of the strange 'burrs' or fossilised trees can be seen as we pass by.

Mupe Bay with its banded rock formations is perhaps the most dramatic of the coastal ledges in Dorset. Our arrival at Mupe, in a little under ½ mile, heralds an unforgettable view that on a clear, but stormy day, is both fearsome and inspiring. If for no other reason, this justifies the hard descent at Lulworth and the even harder ascent that follows. It's time for a rest.

The footpath rounds Mupe Bay before making its ascent. The summit of Radar Hill is furnished with a seat that will prove most welcome!

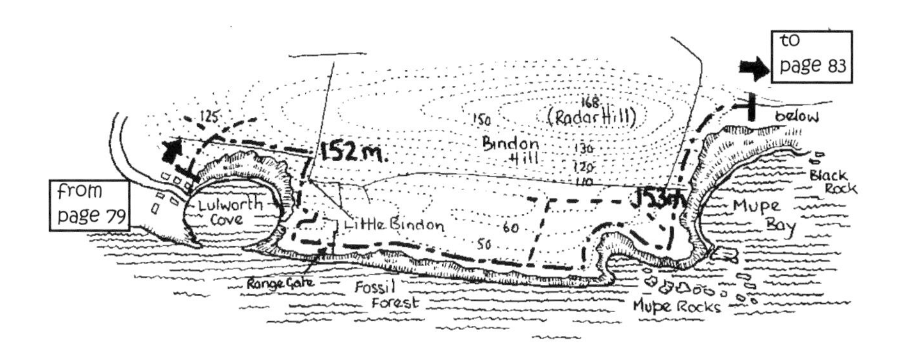

Throughout the Jurassic period (beginning approximately 210 million years ago and lasting for 70 million years), Dorset lay under a tropical sea in which clays, sandstones and limestones formed. Near the end of the Jurassic sea levels dropped, soils developed and trees grew, but as the waters rose once more the forest was drowned under a salt lagoon. Algae then grew across the floor of the lagoon and around the base of the trees. Mud encased the layers of algae and the tree stumps hardened into a limestone band, forming doughnut shaped structures known as burrs. Where the trees once stood the Fossil Forest remains.

The burrs of the fossil forest

From the seat on Radar Hill, walk to the east and begin the descent into the delightfully named bay of Arish Mell.

Certain features will arrest your attention on the descent to the bay. Firstly the many battered tanks and assorted military vehicles that litter the heath below. Secondly Lulworth Castle to the north, and then the muscle-wrenching climb out of the bay to Rings Hill that awaits us. But finally, in the far north east, most significant of all to the 'A Round Dorset' walker, a glimpse of Poole Harbour and journey's end.

A Shelled Tank on the Gunnery Ranges
Arish Mell.

The climb up from Arish Mell is punishing by any standards, but will soon be over. As you near what appears to be the summit, branch off half left towards the stile and star post that signals your arrival at Flowers Barrow, a coastal Iron Age hill fort. Its entrance is found by climbing to the right, then up and across the ring and ditch earthwork.

The eastern-most part the summit of the hill fort, is a more popular picnic area that over looks Worbarrow Bay and Worbarrow Tout being sheltered from the wind between two of the outer banks. From here, cross half left to the gap in the earthwork. A stone way marker confirms our route to Whiteway Car park (1½ miles). It is from here we deviate once more from the Coastal path to follow a wonderful inland ridge. It is the chalk ridge that takes us into the Purbeck Hills and to Corfe Castle and if we were to stay on it, would ultimately conclude at Handfast Point and the Old Harry Rocks.

Worbarrow Bay and Worbarrow Tout
From Flower's Barrow.

Flower's Barrow is a small Iron Age hill fort balanced precariously on the cliff top overlooking Worbarrow Bay and the atmospheric, deserted village of Tyneham. (This stronghold of the Durotriges was probably overrun, along with many other hill forts, by the invading Romans around 43AD).

The southern part of the site has fallen victim to gravity and one can't help feeling that to hang around is to risk being part of the next phase of erosion. The exposed areas have however benefited archaeologists who have recovered artefacts and remains that would have otherwise remained hidden, amongst them an abnormally tall skeleton. Height is not a problem here however; it is a breezy spot with great views even for those of us with legs that only just reach the ground!

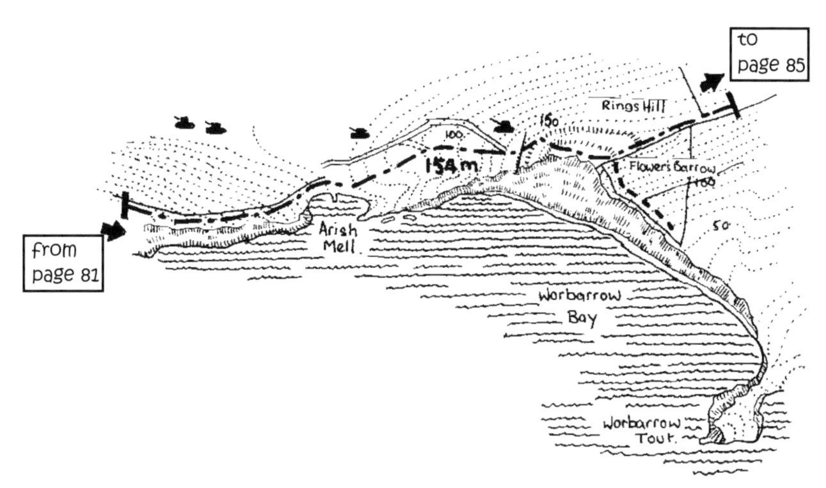

The name Worbarrow means 'hill where watch was kept', from the Old English 'weard' and 'beorg', a description reinforced by the later addition of Tout, meaning 'look-out hill' from the Old English 'tote' or 'tuten'.

The South West From Flower's Barrow.

The stony chalk track across Whiteway Hill is clear and straight. After 1 mile, it comes alongside the minor range road from East Lulworth. Over a stile, there is a wide track going down to the abandoned village of Tyneham on the right.

(If you plan a trip down to the village, you will need to return to this point or follow the minor road to the junction at West Creech Hill.)

The main route continues on the track ahead, alongside the road up to the grass parking area at Povington Hill. Cross the parking area to the far left corner. Go through the gate and continue ahead keeping to the left of the field.

The path enters a small wooded section and there meets the road coming up from Tyneham. Cross the road to a second stile and then follow the path to the left. Cross a third stile to the fenced path that runs along the top of a field with extensive views south across the valley towards Swyre Head with the hamlet of Steeple below.

The path ends at a gate alongside the military guard post that marks the end of the gunnery ranges. At the bend in the road, cross over to the grassy area that leads to a car park and viewpoint.

In the far left corner of the car park, a gate continues the ridge path on to Creech Hill, shortly to arrive at the Grange Arch. This is not so much a folly, but an 'eye catcher' to enhance the view from Creech Grange, the house below the hill to the North. Mr Denis Bond, the then owner of the Grange, built the arch in 1745. The arch also served as a frame for a 'living picture' of the landscape looking back towards and beyond Creech Grange. It still does.

Grange Arch.

Continue along the top of the ridge still in the company of the wooded area (with the rather grandiose title of Great Wood) to your left. At a gate, continue ahead, now in clearer descending ground with just a fence on the left. On springy turf and with extensive views to the south, (that's the Clavel Tower on the skyline, above Kimmeridge Bay) walking is a pleasure to the feet and eyes.

After a ¼ mile or less, turn through a gate on your left and continue with the fence now on your right and a deepening valley on the left, as it descends along a clear track down to a minor road above Stonehill Down.

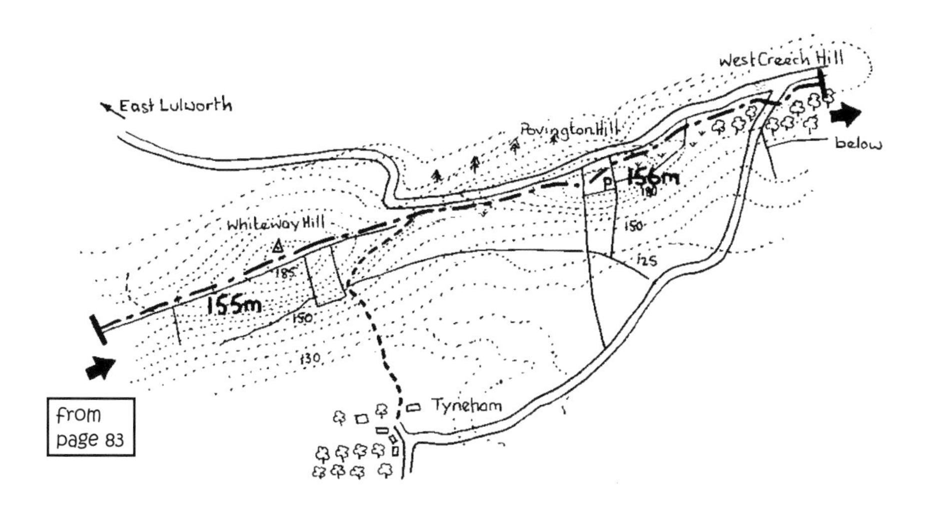
East Lulworth
Povington Hill
West Creech Hill
below
156m
180
150
125
Whiteway Hill
185
155m
150
130
Tyneham
from
page 83

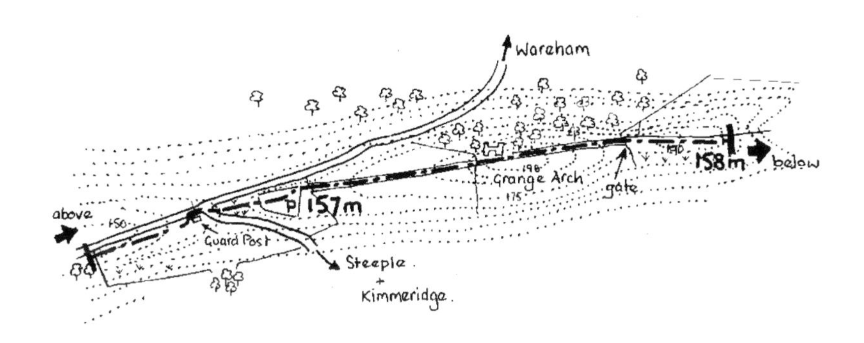
Wareham
above
150
Guard Post
157m
Steeple
+
Kimmeridge
196
Grange Arch
175
gate
190
158m
below

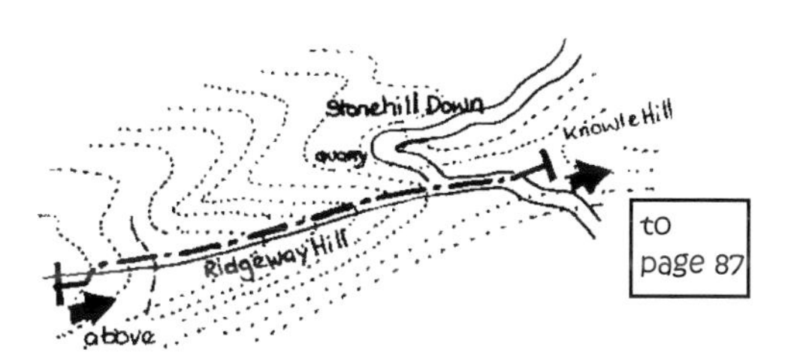
Stonehill Down
quarry
Knowle Hill
Ridgeway Hill
above
to
page 87

Walk along the road for a short distance and as it turns down the hill, leave it to continue ahead on a clear track climbing steadily on to Knowle Hill. Walking soon becomes easy on a high ridge above the village of Church Knowle. The larger village of Corfe Castle lies ahead with the high ground of Challow Hill and Nine Barrow Down beyond it. To the southeast (half right) you can see the church in Kingston.

Knowle Hill.

Beyond the Mary Baxter Memorial Stone, go through the gate then alongside a fence to a second gate. After another 200 yards, a path descends half right to the Underhill Path into Corfe. It is along this path, after emerging from an area of overhanging trees and scrub that the Castle slowly comes into view. Of the many ruined castles in Britain, Corfe must rank among the most dramatic. Standing high on a natural hill, it never ceases to impress. For the next fifteen minutes the camera will be clicking. Corfe is another icon of Dorset and is a high point of the 'A Round Dorset Walk'.

The path ends at a gate below the castle. Don't immediately turn on to the road, but turn slightly left, paralleling the road, to a wooden footbridge over a stream that serves as a moat to the castle itself.

At the road, cross over to a little path than runs around the base of the castle and into the village itself. It's a journey in time and fantasy and is the most perfect introduction to Corfe.

You emerge, blinking and a little bewildered, between stone cottages, alongside the castle entrance and tearooms, into the very heart of a definitive Purbeck village. On high days and holidays it is a bustling place, a magnet to the sightseer, and thus able to provide all that the walker needs for his or her comfort. But the Castle dominates all.

Corfe Castle from the "Underhill Path".

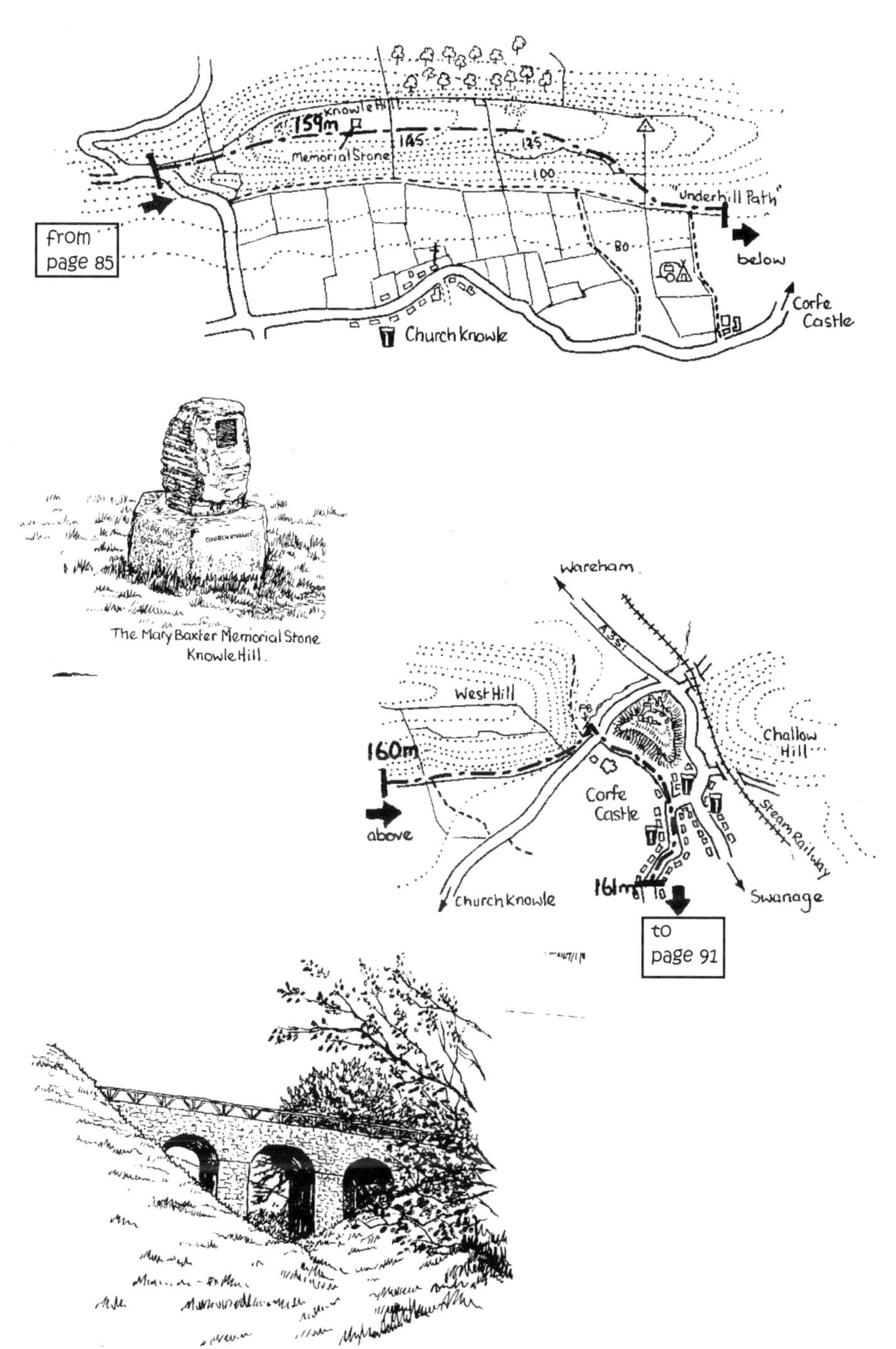

The Mary Baxter Memorial Stone Knowle Hill.

The bridge spanning the ditch between the Inner Gatehouse and the Castle Mound.

It is believed that the Romans first used Corfe Castle's remarkable location as a defensive position. By the 9th century a wooden castle was sited here. The building of the castle that now stands in ruins was begun in the 11th century.

By the 13th century King John had extended the castle both in terms of its fortification and its accommodation. Henry VIII added further walls and towers. In 1572 Queen Elizabeth I sold Corfe to her dancing master, Sir Christopher Hatton and in 1635 the castle was sold to Sir John Bankes, the then Lord Chief Justice.

The English Civil war saw most of Dorset come under the control of the Parliamentarians and by 1643, following the death of Sir John, Corfe Castle, still a stronghold of the Royalist cause, began to endure a series of assaults and sieges. In 1645 a final siege led by a Colonel Bingham finally proved decisive and the Castle was taken, but only through the work of a spy working on the inside. Corfe's obvious defensive position rendered treachery the only viable means by which it could fall. The steepness of its hill must have rendered any conventional attack a daunting prospect.

Following the fall of the Castle, it was mined and destroyed in order that it might not fall once more in to the hands of the Cavaliers, and once again pose such a threat to the Roundhead or Parliamentarian cause.

A trip to the model village in the centre of Corfe Castle (the village) will help to give a clear impression of the castle in its hey day.

In 1880 George Burt (we will be meeting this gentleman a little later), succeeded in getting a bill before parliament for a main railway link to Swanage avoiding the centre of Wareham.

In January 1972 however, British Railways closed the line and lifted the entire track system. However, a group of enthusiasts got together to rebuild the line and in the summer of 1975 a licence was granted to the Swanage Railway Society to occupy the disused Swanage station site and they began its reconstruction as a labour of love.

Initially the track was re-laid as far as Herston, on the outskirts of Swanage, and then onward the three miles to the village of Harman's Cross.

In 1995 the extensions to Corfe Castle and then Norden were completed, and by September 2002 the first through train from the main line at Wareham visited Swanage. The Swanage Railway now runs a daily service between Swanage and Norden, passing through Corfe Castle. For any railway buffs this may be an opportunity too good to waste, but don't be tempted to get a lift to Swanage and thereby avoid a bit of a walk. You are only cheating yourself!

Information on the railway, and all schedules and special events, can be found on their website (www.swanagerailway.co.uk).

Corfe Castle – Swanage (12 miles)

It may be with some reluctance that you leave Corfe. But do so via West Street passing the model village and the Fox Inn, a tavern with character. West Street is the quiet part of Corfe and if you stop and turn around from time-to-time it affords a timeless picture of the castle. At its conclusion some ½mile to the south, cross the cattle grid and head ¼left away from the road, across what may be wet ground. The route is initially indistinct but soon descends to more boggy ground and a series of plank bridges that serve to keep your boots dry and confirm the route ahead. Once over the boggy ground start climbing to the highest point ahead and what appears to be a 'summit' tumulus. This is Corfe Common.

Continue past the tumulus to a post on the skyline then turn to the right on a slightly clearer path along the ridge of the hill. As the path begins to turn back towards Corfe, start angling to your left, keeping to the ridge, and start to look for a large block of Purbeck stone lying on the grass. It serves as a good marker, showing where to begin the descent into the valley below. Walk a few yards past it, and then start angling down, past the gorse bushes, to where you should find a gate hidden among the trees. It leads to a small stone bridge, two stiles, a second little footbridge (wooden) until finally you emerge into a field.

Once in the field, ascend ½ left across two fields with the church in Kingston to the right of our line of walk. Descend to the muddy corner of the field to a small stone bridge, beyond which we must pick our way along a narrow track (A 'drongway' in Dorset dialect) as it begins to rise again to a stile and open field.

Head to the far left corner of the field, to a stile that leads on to the track to Lynch Farm and cross the track to the stile opposite. Head up the small field to its top left corner and another stile. Cross the next field ¼ left, in the direction of the church, to the next corner. Through the metal gate, turn to the right on a well established track lined with wild garlic.

Continue ahead and at a crossing of major tracks turn to the left to the junction of the road from the village of Kingston and The Scott Arms, a pub with the most stunning views of Corfe. If the Scott Arms has no part in your itinerary, turn to the right and in a hundred yards or so start looking for a track on the left signposted to Houns Tout. The track is clear, wide and tree-lined heading almost south.

West Street. Corfe Castle.

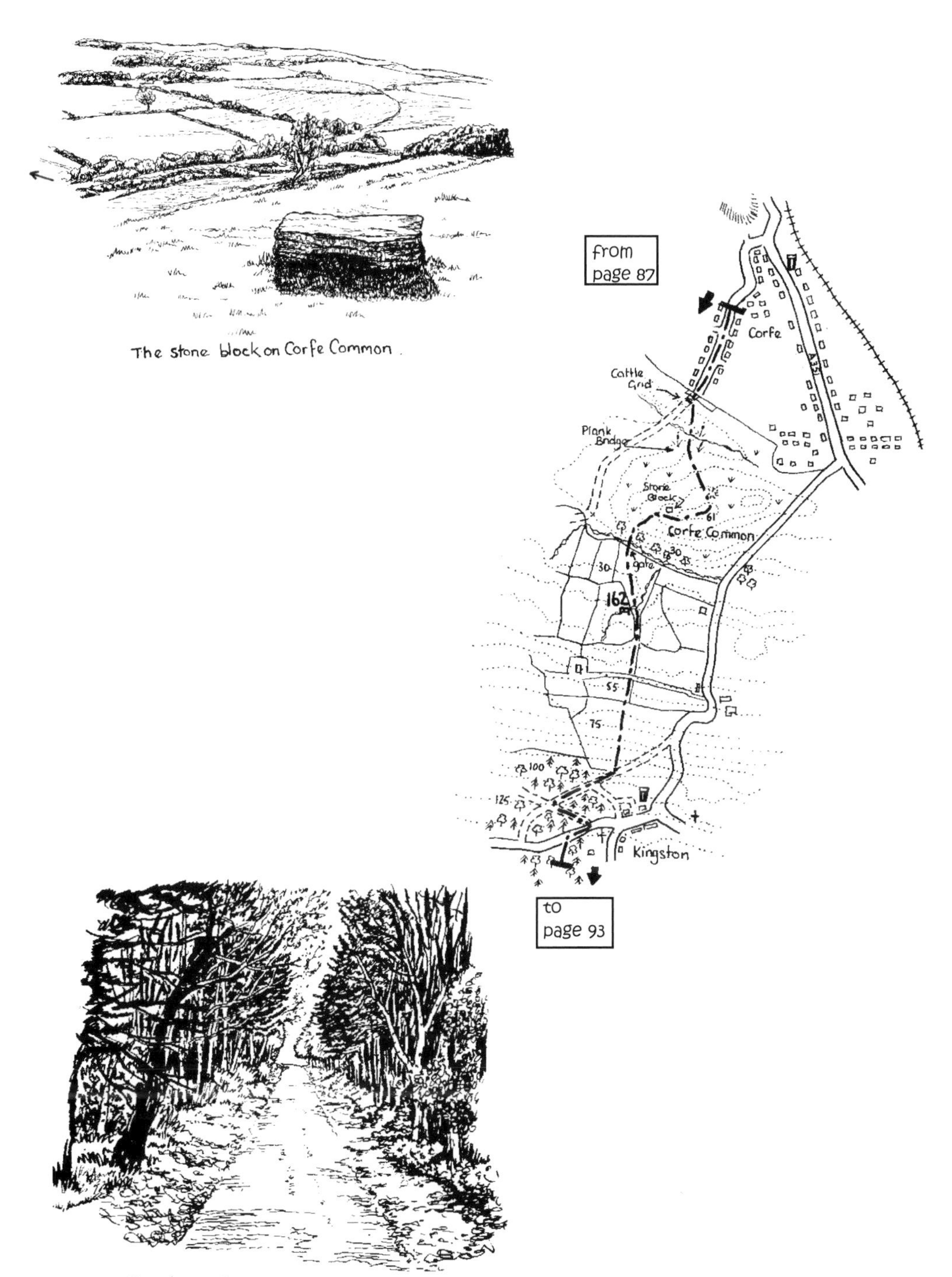

The track from Kingston to Houns-Tout.

After a ¼ mile the track from Kingston meets another track before it bends to the right towards Encombe House. At this point take a lesser path, climbing slightly, half left in front of a cottage offering produce for sale in season. This path leads to a stile and gate and so to clearer ground opening up the view across to Swyre Head, and the valley in which rests Encombe House. You will enjoy this next mile as it heads towards the coast and the resumption of the coastal footpath.

At Houns-Tout take a short rest at the stone seat before turning left on the coastal path with the sea on your right. The way remains clear as it approaches the steep descent to the bay that is Chapman's Pool. Beyond the last of the steps, turn left over a stile and, following the signposts, turn left again almost back upon yourself along the valley below West Hill Wood.

The stile to Hill Bottom from Chapman's Pool. At the foot of Houns-Tout.

Over a stile on a slight rise, turn to the right back towards the east and Hill Bottom. It is tempting along here to avoid the valley altogether and cut directly east towards the high ground of Emmetts Hill. Don't do that, instead continue to turn to the left alongside a fence to head up the next valley terminated by a little community. You will be amply rewarded for the extra half mile walked. When you meet a partially metalled surface alongside Hill Bottom Cottage, turn to the right and descend to a metal gate beyond which, turn right on to a rough track heading back up the valley. The track soon divides. At this point go half left on grass, ascending West Hill along a lesser, sheltered, valley which will, in due course return us to the cliff top along the summit of Emmetts Hill. A stone table and seating has been provided by the Royal Marines as a memorial to those lost since the Second World War. It makes for an excellent place to rest

St Aldhelm's Head (sometimes called St Alban's Head) now looms large, but sadly before the ascent, height must first be lost. (What goes up must first go down). What then follows is a lung-sapping and muscle-breaking climb on steps, with treads and risers not ergonomically designed for the normal gait. There is no point complaining. In any case the view at the top is worth the effort. A stone seat at the summit, offers a welcome relief. It is movingly dedicated to Max Robertson, just eight days old.

St Aldhelm's Head is our most southerly point and a real landmark for the 'A Round Dorset' walker. From here our sights become set on a changing coastline and the return of the Isle of Wight to our horizon, as it was those many days before when we walked together along the promenades of Poole Bay and Bournemouth.

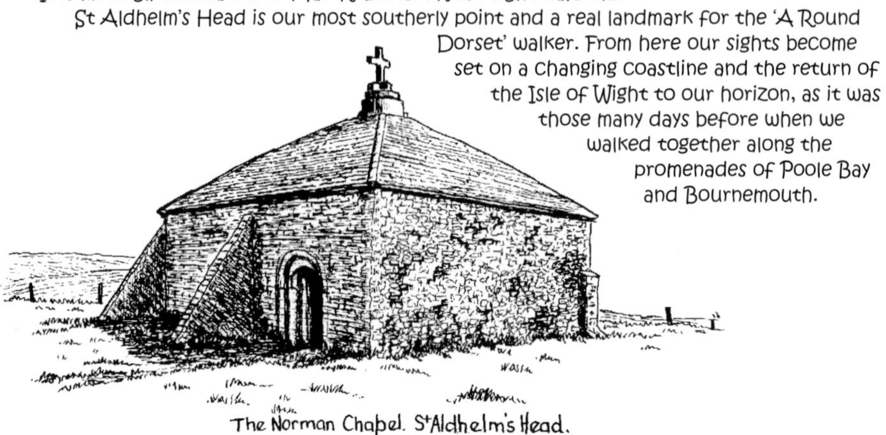

The Norman Chapel. StAldhelm's Head.

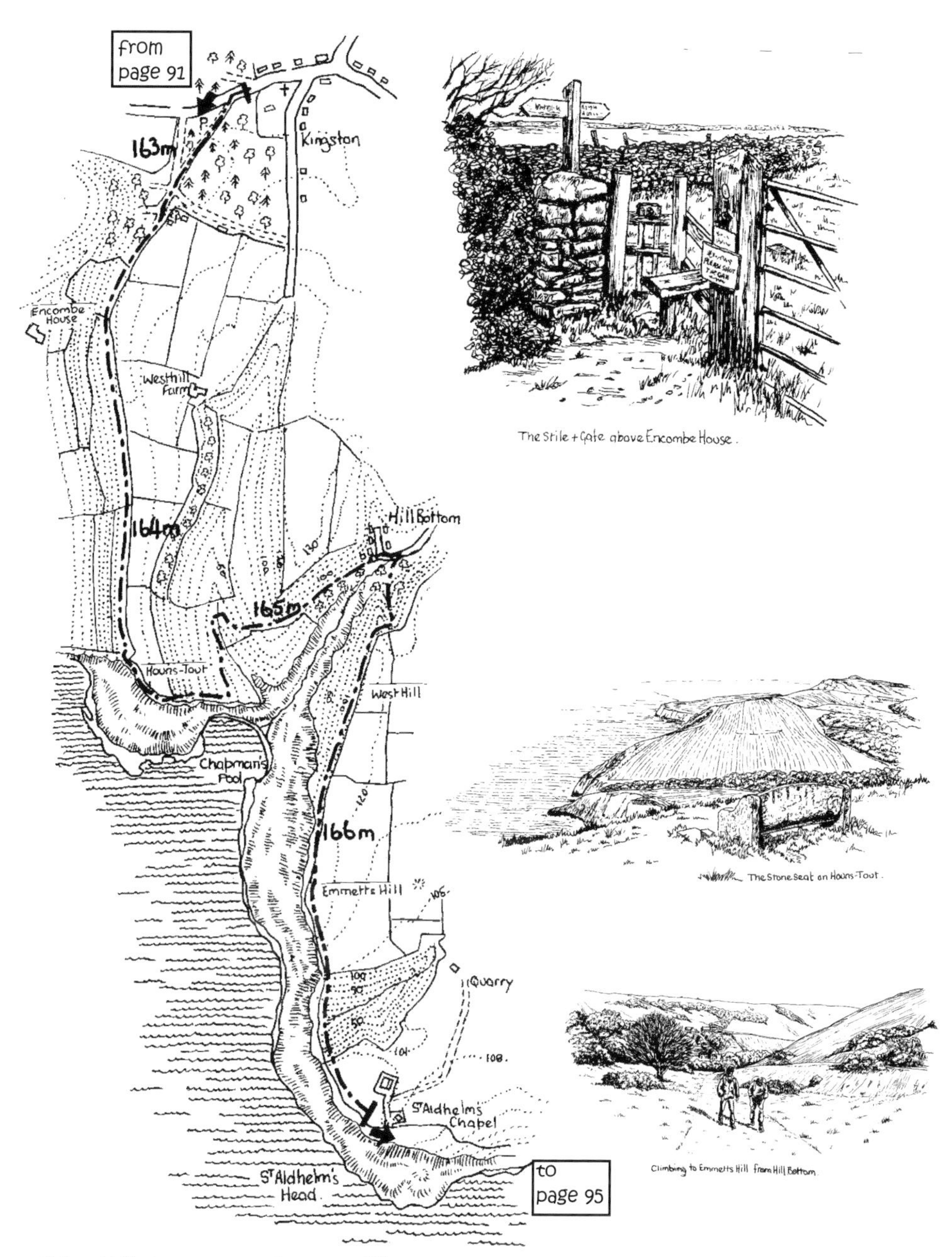

The Stile + Gate above Encombe House.

The Stone Seat on Houns-Tout.

Climbing to Emmetts Hill from Hill Bottom

Saint Aldhelm was a teacher, early Bible translator, evangelist and Abbot of Malmesbury and was appointed the first Bishop of Sherborne in 705 AD. The oddly shaped Norman chapel that bears his name stands in a rare early Christian enclosure. Its unusual shape and heavy construction has led some to believe that it once supported a more substantial structure, perhaps a beacon of some sort?

The look-out station of the National Coast Watch Institution is worth a visit if it is in use. They offer a warm reception and I commend their hospitality.

Winspit.

The route now begins its gentle descent to Winspit alongside a fence and along a path that shows signs of erosion. This has prompted the need for new paths that encroach further into the neighbouring fields. Winspit is reached along the edge and above the quarry itself. This is an obvious place to take a break, with shelter from the wind if it is needed, and much to explore. To stand on the ledges, cut so that the blocks of limestone could be lowered on to barges below, and to regard the galleries cut into the rock face, both here and further down the coast at Seacombe and the Tilly Whim caves, is to gain a graphic insight into the industry that once dominated the coast line hereabouts. Winspit is also the point of access to the archetypal Purbeck village of Worth Matravers, with its fishpond, tearoom and pub (The Square & Compass, perhaps one of the most remarkable pubs in England) 1 mile to the north.

½ mile beyond Winspit, the path turns inland above the valley of Seacombe Bottom. At a stile, turn right, go down the steps, and turn right to return to the cliff path along the landward side of a barbed wire fence.

A further area of quarrying is passed on the way to Dancing Ledge, this is Hedbury Quarry (check out the shipwrecked cannon, you may even get a glimpse of puffins if the time of year is right). The first view of Dancing Ledge is again from above but it will be hard to avoid descending to the flat area cut from the rock that gives the feature its name. Here a curiosity is found in the form of a bathing pool carved out of the rock by quarry-men in the 1890s. (See text on the next page).

Dancing Ledge.

On the way towards Blacker's Hole and Anvil Point the landscape and path change subtly, characterised by meandering through scrub and irregular lumps and bumps. Beyond Blacker's Hole the first of two pairs of metal masts will be passed, the second being just beyond Anvil Point. These served as mile markers for warships involved in speed trials out of Weymouth Harbour.

Before the open area that heralds the lighthouse at Anvil Point (built in 1881), we enter the area defined as Durlston Country Park. We will be in its carefully managed, but attractive, precincts until we reach the outer limits of Swanage.

Walk to the seaward side of the lighthouse on a clear, rocky footpath. The path soon begins to descend towards the caves or galleries of Tilly Whim. The unstable character of these rocks has made the caves unsafe, so continue to their left to the path that climbs above them on a rocky causeway. After this it becomes a carefully prepared surface with a limestone wall on the seaward side. The path soon leads past the abandoned tourist entrance to the caves that were for so long a major attraction.

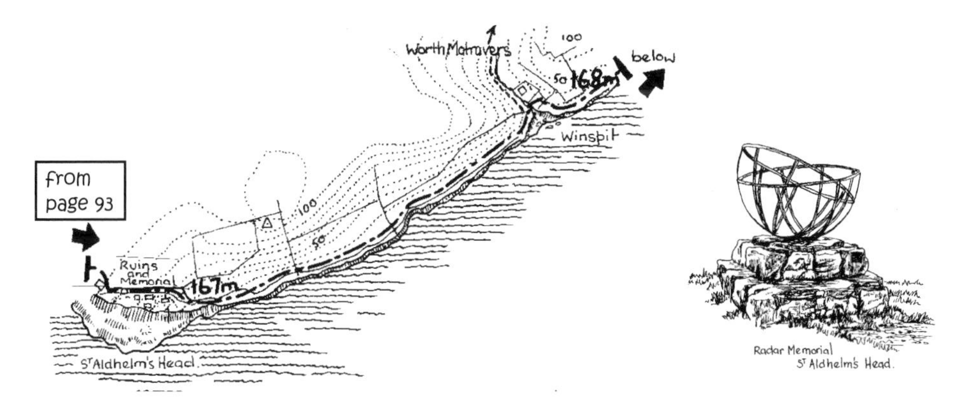

Radar Memorial
St Aldhelm's Head.

Beyond the Coastal watch station, two features recall the development of radar systems here during the last world war There is a new memorial and below it, on a ledge, the ruined remains of the radar station once sited here. (Note also the delicately balanced rock left there by quarry-men with time on their hands.)

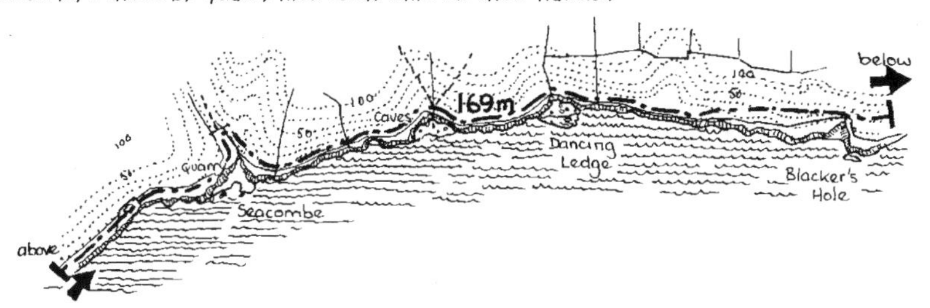

The pool at dancing Ledge was meant for the students of Durnford School, a mile away in Langton Matravers, in order that they could be marched there winter and summer by their headmaster, one Thomas Pellat, for a character-building swim. Whatever Mr Pellat's motives, he wouldn't get away with it today. No sir!

The Tilly Whim Caves

The path continues beyond the caves, closely hugging the cliff edge and offering glimpses of the sea at 140 feet below. The stone wall that stands between you and that sheer drop is a great comfort.

There is a lot to hold the interest along this section, the next being a wooded hut that serves as a dolphin watch point. Inside there is information regarding some of the areas more exotic visitors, in particular porpoises and bottle-nosed dolphins.

The path soon meets a fork, the main route to the right and a turning up to Durlston Castle on the left. (The castle is in fact a folly built in 1887 by an eccentric stone mason named George Burt, who Thomas Hardy called the 'King of Swanage'). The castle now serves as a restaurant, café and tourist centre. Apparently George Burt acquired elements of the castle, including three granite pillars, from 'surplus' artefacts from the building of Trafalgar Square. Below the 'castle' is the Stone Globe. This is a stunning example of both a mason's skill and Burt's eccentricity. It is over 3 metres in diameter and depicts the key features of the earth. It is surrounded by some of the carved inscriptions so loved by George Burt.

The Great Globe Durlston

Back on the main path, the Castle is rounded to an access road. Almost immediately turn to the right along a shady path beneath evergreen oaks. The O.S. map suggests the continuation of this path along the cliff edge. However, if like me you find yourself passing a green area on your left with a cruciform stone seat at its centre, and beyond that you emerge on to a suburban roadway, don't worry. Turn to the right and in a hundred yards or so, signposted to the coastal footpath, turn to the right again on to Belle Vue Road.

As the crescent turns back to the main road, take another right onto the footpath leading to the grassy cliff top of Peveril Point, overlooking the car parks and rooftops of Swanage to the left. Keep to the top of the 'field' until it descends to the roadway, and then head off down the road, past the lifeboat station, towards the pier and numerous holiday attractions that constitute the 'Swanage experience'. Here pubs, fish and chip shops and 'kiss me quick hats' abound!

Swanage from Peverill Point

Mrs King requested I inform the ornithologists among you that the Durlston Country Park Visitor's Centre is especially worth a visit. Cameras have been positioned in order that nesting sites of some of the more interesting birds can be monitored in comfort. Is that all right now Mrs K?

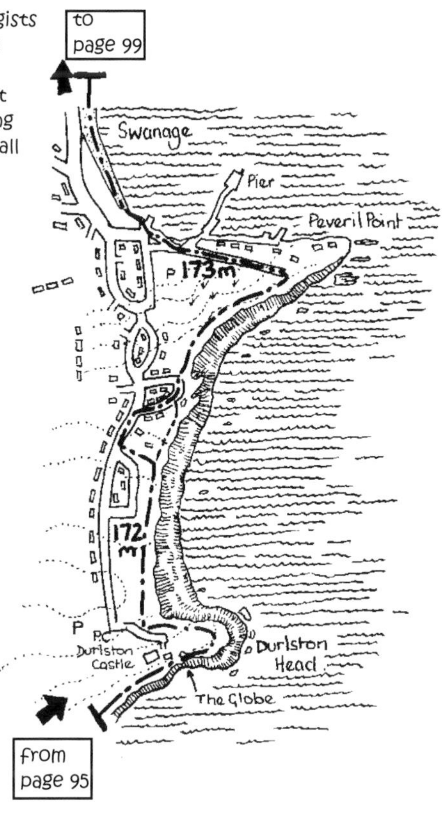

Whilst the word 'Tilly' in Tilly Whim apparently relates to one of the quarrymen, 'whim' comes from the name of the derricks or cranes that were used to lower limestone blocks on to the barges that transported the limestone to the port in Swanage.

The abandoned entrance to the Tilly Whim Caves

The caves were closed to the public in 1976 following some rock falls. They now offer a home to hibernating bats. The particular type of limestone that made Purbeck Stone so popular was called Purbeck Freestone. Apart from its use in many of London's major building works, it was also much in demand during the Napoleonic wars for the building of fortifications along the coast. After 1815 the need declined. An information board alongside the caves reminds us of one obvious but sobering thought. The quarrying that created the vast network of channels and chambers lying beneath our feet, and the blocks of stone removed from them, (often as large as 15 tons apiece), are all the result of work completed with the most basic of hand tools.

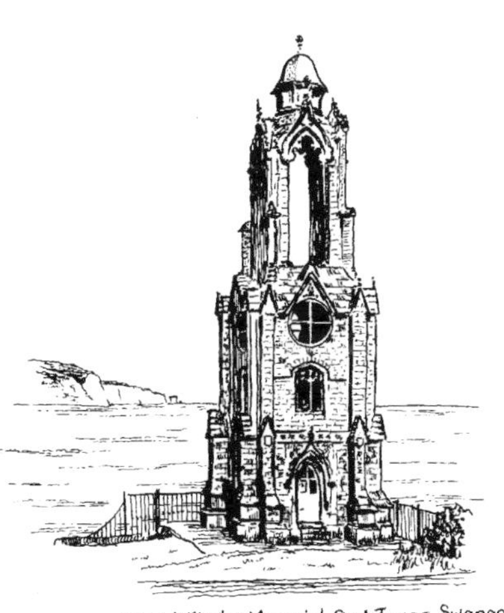

The Wellington Memorial Clock Tower, Swanage.

Swanage to Haven Point (8 miles)

I suspect that for most 'A Round Dorset walkers', Swanage will mark the starting point for the final push and the last stage in our circumnavigation of the county. For that reason alone the walk north along Shore Road alongside the beach, will be especially memorable.

The headland, from Ballard Down towards Ballard Point, dominates the skyline and is itself our first target. To reach it we must first continue our march along Shore Road that becomes renamed Ulwell Road as it begins to turn away from the beach.
After a ¼ mile Ulwell Road bends to the left. Just beyond the bend, turn right (thereby re-establishing a northerly course) on to Redcliff Road. As Redcliff Road bends to the left turn right on to Hill Road. Ever determined to maintain that direct route to Ballard Down, at the next left bend continue ahead on a narrow track, climbing gently towards Whitecliff Farm.

Beyond the roadway (to the farm on the right) continue ahead on to a narrow tree-lined path that, beyond a gate, begins to climb half right up on to the open hillside.

The climb up on to Ballard Down, though steep, is not arduous and the views back to Swanage compensate well for the effort. The path along the summit ridge is joined alongside a fence. Here turn to the right and enjoy the gentle descent, on grassland, towards Ballard Point. In spite of all the other pleasures to the senses this part of the walk provides, more than one glance will turn to the North, for from this last lofty position of the round Dorset walk, the end can be seen i.e. Haven Point and even perhaps the ferry itself. We have waited a long time to take a ride on that worthy vessel.

Old. Harry Rocks. Handfast Point.

Beyond a gate and trig point the path from Ballard Down begins to veer to the left and to draw closer to the precipitous white cliffs that stretch to the northwest from Ballard Point to Hand Fast Point and the Old Harry Rocks. The collection of eroded stacks and stumps, that comprise the Old Harry Rocks, does not come into view until quite late, at a point where the path comes precariously close to cliff edge. This stretch of cliff-top is known as Old Nick's Ground.

At the very tip of Handfast Point, the path thankfully turns to the left to begin the gentle ¾ mile descent into the village of Studland. The track is wide and clear, made so by the passage of many feet. After ½ mile, continue through a gate and carry on down to the tarmac road at a bend and alongside public conveniences. (On the descent from Handfast Point, shortly after the gate, a footpath on the right provides an alternative route via the beach, but it is an unnecessary diversion unless you want to paddle for a while. There will be plenty of opportunities for paddling later.

At the roadway then, turn to the right up Manor Road towards the Bankes Arms. This is the very last watering hole on our Round Dorset Walk. If for no other reason, I feel that makes a stop here obligatory. The final three miles is a gentle stroll along the sands and if time is not a problem, the Bankes Arms is surely the place for a celebratory glass.

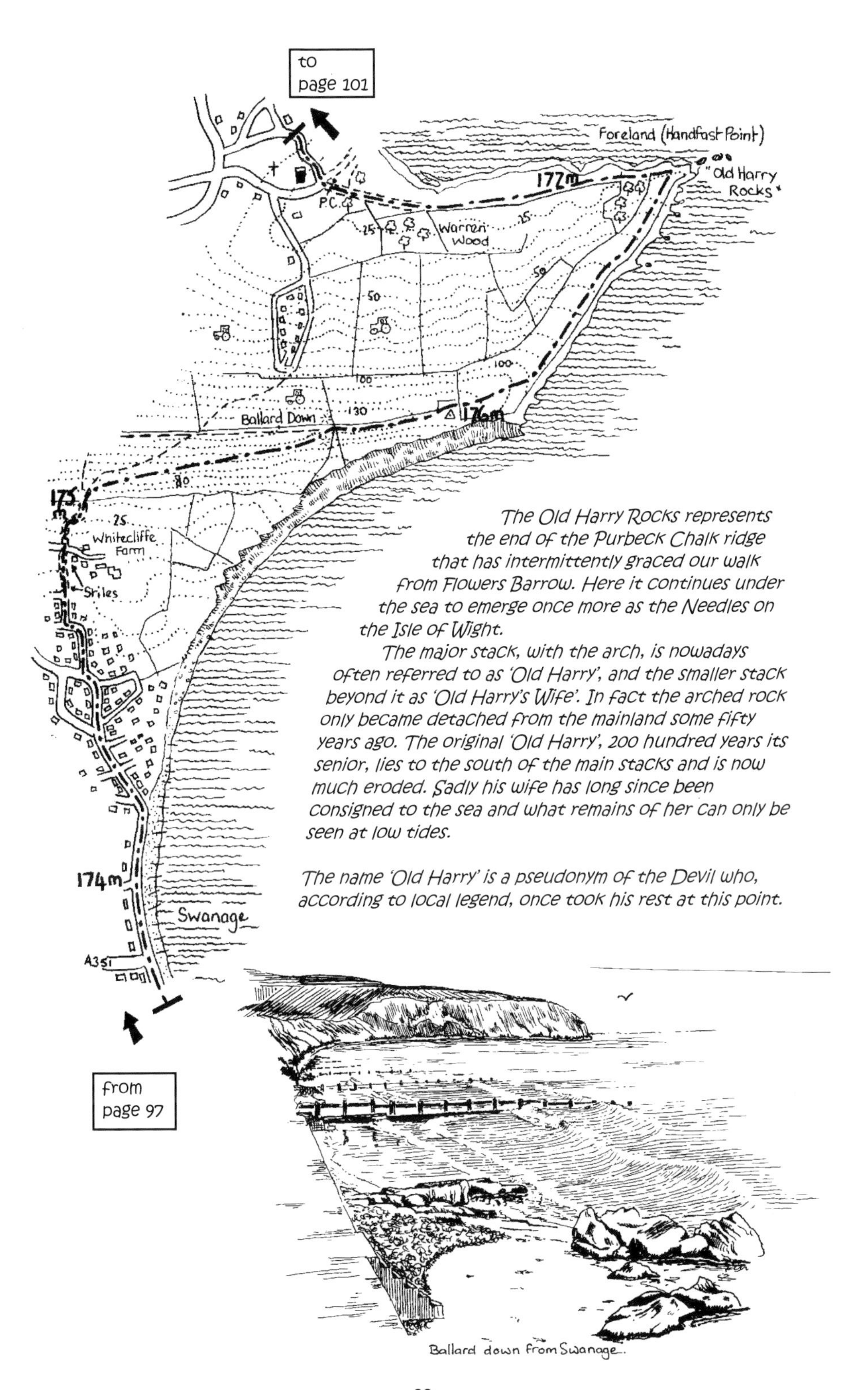

The Old Harry Rocks represents the end of the Purbeck Chalk ridge that has intermittently graced our walk from Flowers Barrow. Here it continues under the sea to emerge once more as the Needles on the Isle of Wight.

The major stack, with the arch, is nowadays often referred to as 'Old Harry', and the smaller stack beyond it as 'Old Harry's Wife'. In fact the arched rock only became detached from the mainland some fifty years ago. The original 'Old Harry', 200 hundred years its senior, lies to the south of the main stacks and is now much eroded. Sadly his wife has long since been consigned to the sea and what remains of her can only be seen at low tides.

The name 'Old Harry' is a pseudonym of the Devil who, according to local legend, once took his rest at this point.

Ballard down from Swanage.

Well, this is it. After some 178 miles, only three remain. How determinedly you start this last leg will no doubt depend upon the length of time spent in the Bankes Arms. But with the task nearly done, it is with a rising sense of anticipation that we set off along Manor Road to the north.

We soon pass the Manor House Hotel on the right. Continue on ahead until you meet Beach Road at a 'T' junction. Here turn to the right to head down to the Beach passing the car park as you do so.

Once at the beach there remains little more for me to say in the way of directions. Keep the sea on your right and the dunes on your left and you cannot go wrong.

The beaches of Studland Bay must possess one of the finest stretches of white sand in the country, yet it remains pretty well unspoilt by the usual seaside developments and commercial exploitation, and for that we must be grateful. Stretches of coastline like this are rare indeed, which is why it is regularly voted as being amongst the finest beaches in the country.

Whilst walking along this stretch (the foreshore close to the water makes for easier walking) don't be surprised if you meet film crews, because of its unspoilt character it is often used as a location for film and television productions. One thing you are more likely to see however, on all but the coldest days, are people frolicking in even less clothing than is customary on an English beach – nudists or as they prefer to be called naturists. There may be a few naturalists as well but you will not necessarily confuse them. Studland Beach has long been used by naturists, but in recent years their presence has been more formally acknowledged and they have been encouraged to remain within certain limits; limits marked by sign posts.

Inland beyond the sand dunes lies an extensive area of heathland which is well worth exploring, but for most I suspect, the pace will increase as the northern end of Studland Bay is approached, for here, as the beach turns to the left into Shell Bay, we are greeted by the sight for which we have worked so long, namely the end; the finish; the goal; the ferry at Haven Point.

Unless you have arranged otherwise, I suspect there will be little in the way of a reception committee here to greet you. As this is also the end of the South Coast Peninsular Footpath, walkers are not an uncommon sight even amongst the usual seaside holidaymakers. Yet you will enjoy, as I did, an exceptional thrill and might even shed a silent tear. You have accomplished a special achievement; you have circumnavigated the county of Dorset under your own steam. As you dip your toes in the water of the channel at Haven Point you will see again the start point you left behind so long ago knowing you can go no further (without going on a lap of honour). The circle is now complete. The job is done, and may I be the first to congratulate you.

Sandbanks Ferry, South Haven.

'We shall not cease from exploration, and the end of all our exploring will be to arrive where we started and know the place for the first time.'
From 'Little Gidding', Four Quartets by T.S. Eliot

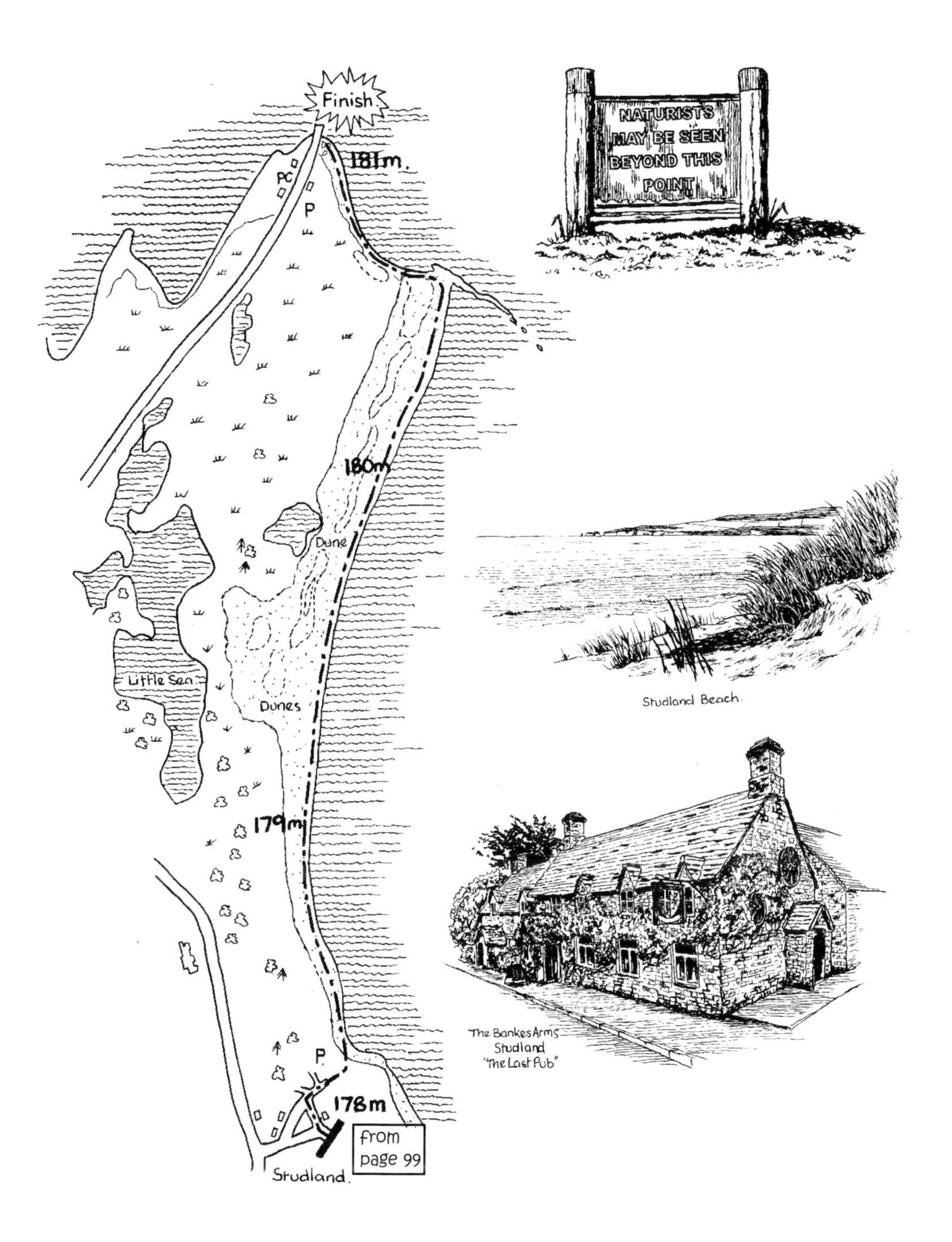

Studland Beach.

The Bankes Arms offers a wide range of real ales and not least among the range are the ales brewed on the premises; those of the 'Isle of Purbeck Brewery', a small brewery that has been brewing here since 2003.

ARound Dorset Walk, Daily Diary

Date	Start Point	Finish Point	Cumulative Mileage	Comments

A Round Dorset Walk, Daily Diary

Date	Start Point	Finish Point	Cumulative Mileage	Comments

A Round Dorset Walk has a website:

www.ARoundDorsetWalk.co.uk

This has been constructed to help you organize your walk around Dorset. It contains some background to the walk and information on accommodation, transport and facilities on route.There are some useful links and, where necessary, any amendments to the route or additional excursions that might enhance your enjoyment of the walk. It also gives you the opportunity to chat with the author.

Hobnob Press publishes books about Wiltshire, Dorset and the surrounding area

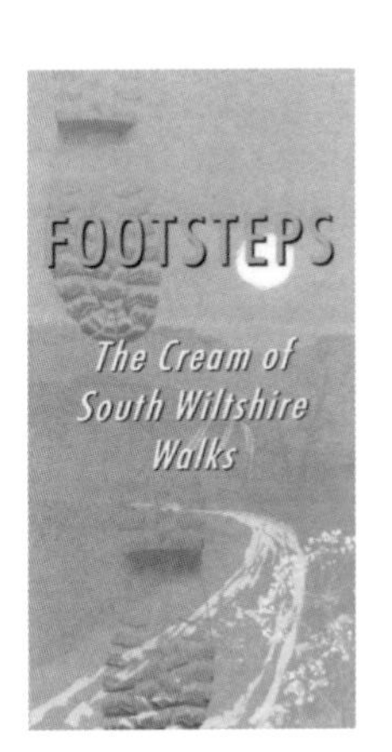

Two other Hobnob books you will enjoy are:
Footsteps: the cream of South Wiltshire Walks - nine well known local authors and writers contribute a total of 17 superb walks of varying lengths. £6.95 paperback, £12.50 hardback.

A Higher Reality, by John Chandler, an absorbing and wide-ranging history of Shaftesbury's royal nunnery, including a walk around the abbey precincts and the town. £7.95 paperback, £9.95 hardback

For details of all Hobnob Press books write to us at PO Box 1838, East Knoyle, Salisbury SP3 6FA, or visit our website:

www.hobnobpress.co.uk